I0017300

AI MACHINE LEARNING SIMPLIFIED A BEGINNER'S GUIDE TO ARTIFICIAL INTELLIGENCE

Practical Techniques for AI, Deep Learning, and Data Science

THOMPSON CARTER

All rights reserved

No part of this book may be reproduced, distributed, or transmitted in any form or by any means without the prior written permission of the publisher, except in the case of brief quotations embodied in critical reviews and certain other noncommercial uses permitted by copyright law.

TABLE OF CONTENTS

INTRODUCTION

Why AI Matters Today

Artificial Intelligence (AI) is no longer a futuristic concept found only in science fiction; it's a reality shaping the world we live in today. From the moment we wake up and check our smartphones to the way we interact with the world, AI plays an invisible yet crucial role in enhancing our daily lives. In this introduction, we will explore how AI impacts everything around us—from our personal devices and apps to critical industries like healthcare, finance, and transportation. We'll also debunk some common myths about AI, providing a clear, accurate picture of what this technology really is and what it isn't. By the end of this book, you'll have a strong foundational understanding of AI and machine learning, equipped with real-world examples to illustrate these powerful technologies.

Overview of the Impact of AI in Daily Life

Think about your typical day. You might wake up, check your phone for the weather, or get a notification reminding you about a meeting. When you sit down for breakfast, perhaps your music app recommends a playlist based on your mood, or your news app curates stories just for you. AI powers each of these interactions.

In *smartphones*, AI is embedded in voice assistants like Siri, Google Assistant, or Alexa. These assistants use **natural language processing (NLP)** to understand and respond to your voice commands. When you ask Siri about the weather, an AI algorithm processes your question, accesses the necessary data, and delivers a response in seconds.

Streaming services like **Netflix, YouTube, and Spotify** use AI-powered recommendation engines. These systems analyze your past behavior, compare it with millions of other users, and suggest movies, videos, or songs you might like next. The AI behind these suggestions is so effective that it often feels like these platforms "know" you better than you know yourself.

Online shopping platforms, such as Amazon, leverage AI to offer personalized product recommendations. Each time you browse or buy a product, AI algorithms learn more about your preferences, making future suggestions more accurate. This not only improves your shopping experience but also drives significant revenue for companies.

Even in everyday tasks like email management, AI plays a key role. Have you ever noticed how Gmail automatically filters spam emails or suggests quick replies? That's AI in action, designed to make communication faster and more efficient.

AI in Industries: Healthcare, Finance, Transportation, and Entertainment

While AI powers many everyday conveniences, its most transformative impact may be in industries like healthcare, finance, transportation, and entertainment. Let's take a look at how AI is revolutionizing each of these sectors.

Healthcare

AI is dramatically changing healthcare by enhancing diagnostic capabilities, improving patient care, and even discovering new treatments. For example, **IBM Watson Health** uses AI to analyze massive datasets of medical literature and patient information to assist doctors in diagnosing diseases like cancer. AI can detect patterns in medical imaging that the human eye might miss, leading to earlier and more accurate diagnoses.

In drug discovery, AI is accelerating the research process. Traditionally, finding new drugs could take years, but AI can quickly analyze thousands of chemical compounds and predict which ones might be effective in treating specific diseases. This capability became especially important during the COVID-19 pandemic, where AI helped accelerate the search for treatments and vaccines.

Finance

In the financial sector, AI is used to optimize trading strategies, manage risk, and detect fraudulent activities. **High-frequency**

trading, where AI algorithms execute thousands of trades in seconds, is now a common practice on Wall Street. These algorithms analyze market trends, historical data, and other inputs faster than any human trader could.

AI is also critical in **fraud detection**. Banks and credit card companies use AI systems to monitor transactions and flag suspicious activities. For instance, if a transaction occurs in a location that doesn't match your usual spending patterns, AI can instantly alert you or block the transaction until it is verified. This kind of real-time analysis reduces the risk of fraud and enhances security for customers.

Transportation

Perhaps one of the most visible and discussed applications of AI is in the development of **self-driving cars**. Companies like **Tesla**, **Waymo**, and **Uber** are investing heavily in autonomous vehicle technology, where AI systems make driving decisions by processing data from cameras, sensors, and radar in real-time. These systems assess road conditions, detect obstacles, and navigate safely through traffic.

Beyond self-driving cars, AI is also used in **traffic management**. AI-powered systems can analyze traffic patterns and predict congestion, allowing city planners to optimize roadways and reduce delays. In logistics and delivery, companies like **Amazon** and **UPS** use AI to route delivery vehicles efficiently, ensuring faster shipping times.

Entertainment

In entertainment, AI has become a powerful tool for content creation and personalization. Streaming services like **Netflix** not only recommend content but also use AI to predict what kinds of shows and movies they should produce next. By analyzing viewing habits and trends, these platforms can anticipate audience preferences and invest in original content that has a higher likelihood of success.

Additionally, AI is used in **video game design**, where it powers intelligent, adaptive opponents that can learn and adjust to player strategies. Games like **Fortnite** and **Call of Duty** use AI-driven characters and environments to create more immersive and dynamic gaming experiences.

Debunking Myths About AI

As AI becomes more integrated into our lives, misconceptions about the technology persist. Let's clear up some of the most common myths:

1. **Myth: AI will replace all human jobs.**
   - **Reality:** While AI may automate certain tasks, it is unlikely to replace all jobs. Instead, AI will create new roles, especially in fields that require human creativity, judgment, and emotional

intelligence. Many industries will see a shift where humans and AI work together, with AI handling repetitive tasks and humans focusing on more complex decision-making.

2. **Myth: AI is as intelligent as humans.**
   o **Reality:** Despite impressive advancements, today's AI is far from achieving **Artificial General Intelligence (AGI)**, or human-level intelligence. AI systems are highly specialized and can only perform tasks they are trained for. They lack the general reasoning and problem-solving abilities of humans.

3. **Myth: AI is a new phenomenon.**
   o **Reality:** AI has been around for decades, with early research dating back to the 1950s. What's new is the vast amount of data and computing power available today, which has accelerated AI's development and real-world applications.

4. **Myth: AI is only for big tech companies.**
   o **Reality:** AI is increasingly accessible to smaller businesses and individuals. Many AI tools and platforms offer user-friendly interfaces, allowing non-experts to integrate AI into their

workflows. As AI technology continues to evolve, it will become even more democratized.

What This Book Will Teach You

By now, you can see that AI is already playing a significant role in many aspects of our lives, from personal conveniences to critical industries. But understanding AI and machine learning doesn't have to be overwhelming. In this book, you will learn:

- The basics of AI and machine learning, explained in simple, jargon-free terms
- The key differences between AI, machine learning, and deep learning
- How machines learn from data and make decisions
- Real-world examples of AI applications across various industries
- The ethical and societal implications of AI, including its limitations and risks

Whether you're completely new to AI or looking to deepen your understanding, this book will give you the tools and knowledge to grasp this transformative technology. Through clear explanations and real-world examples, we'll break down complex topics into manageable pieces, ensuring you walk away with a solid foundation in AI and machine learning.

Conclusion   to   the   Introduction

AI is no longer a concept of the future; it's here, influencing almost every aspect of modern life. This book will demystify AI, explaining how it works, why it matters, and how it's changing industries and daily activities. As you move through the chapters, you'll not only understand the technology but also see how AI impacts you personally—and why it's so important to stay informed about its advancements. Ready to dive in? Let's get started!

CHAPTER 1: WHAT IS ARTIFICIAL INTELLIGENCE?

Artificial Intelligence (AI) has become a buzzword in today's world, often associated with futuristic robots, self-driving cars, and machines that seem capable of thinking like humans. But what exactly is AI? In this chapter, we'll define AI in simple terms, explore its history, clarify the difference between AI, machine learning, and deep learning, and provide real-world examples of AI applications, like chatbots and virtual assistants.

Defining AI in Simple Terms

At its core, **Artificial Intelligence (AI)** refers to the ability of machines or computers to mimic human intelligence. This could include tasks like learning from experience, recognizing patterns, making decisions, understanding language, or solving problems. When we say a system has AI, it means that it can perform functions that normally require human intelligence.

Think about how humans learn: we observe, process information, and then use what we've learned to make decisions. AI tries to do the same, except machines learn through data, algorithms, and patterns rather than through experience as humans do. Importantly, AI is not a singular technology but an umbrella term that encompasses a range of tools and methods used to create "intelligent" behavior in machines.

In simple terms: AI allows computers to perform tasks that typically require human-like thinking or problem-solving, but instead of understanding the world like we do, they rely on data and predefined rules.

A Brief History: From Early Computers to Modern AI

The history of AI dates back much further than many people realize. Let's walk through some key moments in its evolution.

The Birth of Computing and the Idea of AI (1940s-1950s)

AI's roots can be traced back to the development of early computers. In the 1940s, the creation of the first digital computers enabled machines to perform calculations at speeds unimaginable to humans. This sparked the question: could machines be made to think?

One of the earliest pioneers in AI was British mathematician and computer scientist **Alan Turing**. In 1950, Turing published a landmark paper titled **"Computing Machinery and Intelligence,"** where he proposed the idea of a machine that could simulate any human intellectual task. Turing's work laid the foundation for AI, and he famously posed the question: "Can machines think?" He also developed the **Turing Test**, a way to measure a machine's ability to exhibit intelligent behavior indistinguishable from that of a human.

The Early Days of AI (1950s-1970s)

In the 1950s and 60s, researchers began to develop early AI programs that could solve mathematical problems, play games like chess, and even perform basic reasoning tasks. One of the first successful AI programs was **The Logic Theorist** (1956), developed by Allen Newell and Herbert A. Simon, which could prove mathematical theorems.

During this time, excitement about AI was high. Researchers thought that within a few decades, machines would achieve human-level intelligence. However, as the complexity of real-world tasks became apparent, progress slowed, leading to a period known as the "AI Winter" in the 1970s, where enthusiasm and funding for AI research declined.

The Rise of Machine Learning (1980s-2000s)

In the 1980s and 90s, AI saw a resurgence, driven largely by advances in **machine learning**—a subfield of AI that focuses on systems that learn from data rather than being explicitly programmed. Machine learning allowed computers to recognize patterns and improve their performance over time.

By the 2000s, advances in computational power and access to large amounts of data led to new breakthroughs in AI, particularly in the areas of speech recognition, image recognition, and language translation. Companies like **Google** and **IBM** started to invest heavily in AI research, leading to the modern AI applications we use today.

Modern AI and Deep Learning (2010s-Present)

In the 2010s, AI development accelerated with the rise of **deep learning**, a type of machine learning that uses artificial neural networks inspired by the human brain. Deep learning made it possible for machines to handle much more complex tasks, such as recognizing objects in images, understanding speech, and even generating human-like text.

Today, AI is embedded in countless applications, from virtual assistants like **Siri** and **Alexa** to self-driving cars, facial recognition, and AI-generated art. The possibilities for AI seem limitless, but there is still much work to be done to achieve human-level general intelligence.

AI vs. Machine Learning vs. Deep Learning

One of the most common points of confusion for beginners is the difference between AI, machine learning, and deep learning. These terms are often used interchangeably, but they refer to distinct concepts.

Artificial Intelligence (AI)

As we've defined earlier, AI is the broadest term. It refers to machines designed to perform tasks that would normally require human intelligence. This could be anything from a basic program that can sort emails to an advanced system like a self-driving car.

Machine Learning (ML)

Machine Learning is a subset of AI. It refers to the idea that machines can "learn" from data without being explicitly programmed for every possible outcome. Instead of following fixed rules, machine learning systems analyze large amounts of data, recognize patterns, and make predictions or decisions based on what they've learned.

For example, in traditional programming, a developer might write specific rules telling a program how to identify spam emails. In machine learning, the system is given thousands of examples of spam and non-spam emails and "learns" to distinguish between them based on patterns it detects in the data.

Deep Learning

Deep Learning is a subset of machine learning that involves neural networks—algorithms modeled loosely after the human brain. Deep learning systems are incredibly powerful and can process vast amounts of unstructured data, such as images, audio, or text.

For example, deep learning is what enables facial recognition technology. A neural network can analyze an image and determine whether it contains a human face, and even identify specific individuals based on their unique facial features.

In summary:

- **AI** is the broad field of creating intelligent systems.
- **Machine learning** is a way for machines to learn from data.
- **Deep learning** is a more advanced form of machine learning that uses neural networks to handle complex tasks.

Real-World Examples: Chatbots, Virtual Assistants, and Automated Customer Service

Now that we've defined AI and its related fields, let's look at some real-world examples that you probably encounter regularly—examples that demonstrate how AI is already a part of our everyday lives.

Chatbots

Chatbots are AI-powered programs that simulate conversations with users, typically through messaging apps or websites. They can answer common customer service questions, assist with tasks like booking appointments, and even provide technical support.

A simple example of a chatbot is the customer service agents you often interact with on websites. These chatbots use **natural language processing (NLP)** to understand customer queries and respond with helpful answers. For instance, if you visit an e-commerce website and ask, "Where's my order?", the chatbot will pull up information about your purchase and provide a status update.

Some advanced chatbots, like **Google's AI-powered chatbot Duplex**, can even make phone calls to book appointments on your behalf, sounding almost indistinguishable from a real human.

Virtual Assistants

Virtual assistants like **Apple's Siri**, **Amazon's Alexa**, and **Google Assistant** are AI systems designed to help users perform tasks using voice commands. These assistants can set reminders, answer questions, control smart home devices, and provide personalized recommendations.

Virtual assistants rely heavily on machine learning and natural language processing to understand user requests. For example, when you ask Alexa to play your favorite song, the assistant analyzes your request, accesses your music library, and plays the song. Over time, virtual assistants also learn your preferences, making future interactions more personalized.

Automated Customer Service

In industries like banking, retail, and telecommunications, AI-driven automated customer service is becoming the norm. When you call a customer service hotline and interact with an automated voice system, you're likely talking to an AI system that uses speech recognition to understand your request and provide relevant information.

For example, many banks now offer AI-powered phone systems that can handle tasks like checking your balance, transferring money, or paying bills—all without the need for a human operator. These systems can resolve common issues quickly and efficiently, saving companies time and resources while improving customer satisfaction.

Conclusion

In this chapter, we've explored what AI is, traced its history from the early days of computing to modern AI, and clarified the differences between AI, machine learning, and deep learning. By understanding these key concepts, you can begin to see how AI is not just a futuristic technology but something that is already shaping the world around us.

Through real-world examples like chatbots, virtual assistants, and automated customer service, AI is increasingly becoming a part of our daily lives. These systems make our lives easier by handling tasks that once required human intervention, offering a glimpse of how AI will continue to evolve in the years to come.

As we move forward in this book, we'll dive deeper into the technical aspects of AI and machine learning, explore more real-world applications, and discuss the ethical challenges AI presents in society. But for now, the foundation has been laid—AI is not as complex or distant as it may seem, and by the end of this book, you'll be equipped with the knowledge to understand and appreciate its role in the modern world.

CHAPTER 2: HOW MACHINES LEARN: AN OVERVIEW OF MACHINE LEARNING (ML)

In the previous chapter, we explored the concept of Artificial Intelligence (AI) and touched briefly on machine learning (ML) as a subset of AI. Now, we'll delve deeper into machine learning itself—how it works, the different types of learning involved, and how this technology drives many of the systems we use every day, like Netflix and YouTube's recommendation engines.

Machine learning is at the heart of modern AI, and understanding it is crucial to grasping how machines can make decisions, recognize patterns, and even improve over time without being explicitly programmed for every scenario. By the end of this chapter, you'll have a clear understanding of what machine learning is, the key types of learning it encompasses, and a real-world example that shows how it influences our everyday lives.

Introduction to Machine Learning in Layman's Terms

At its most basic, **machine learning** is the science of getting computers to learn from data. Unlike traditional programming, where a developer explicitly writes instructions for every task, machine learning enables a system to "figure things out" by itself based on the data it's fed. The more data it has, the better it gets at making predictions or decisions.

Imagine you're teaching a child how to identify animals. You wouldn't explain every detail about each animal; instead, you'd show them pictures of cats, dogs, and other animals. Over time, the child would learn to recognize patterns—like the shape of ears, the length of tails, or the sound an animal makes—to tell the difference between a cat and a dog. That's essentially what machine learning does, except it uses large datasets and algorithms instead of real-world pictures.

In simple terms: **Machine learning is a method of teaching computers to learn from data, recognize patterns, and make decisions or predictions based on that data.**

Machine learning works because of the vast amount of digital data we now generate and collect. The more data we provide, the more accurate machine learning systems become. This is why companies like Google, Amazon, and Facebook have been able to develop highly sophisticated AI systems: they have access to enormous amounts of user data that they can use to train their models.

Let's look at a basic machine learning process:

1. **Input data** is provided to the system (e.g., images of animals).

2. **The algorithm** processes the data and tries to recognize patterns or relationships (e.g., features that make a dog different from a cat).

3. **The system makes predictions** based on what it has learned (e.g., this is likely a cat because it has certain characteristics).

4. **The system improves** over time as it receives more data and adjusts its model to become more accurate (e.g., after seeing more cats and dogs, it gets better at distinguishing between them).

Types of Machine Learning: Supervised, Unsupervised, and Reinforcement Learning

Machine learning can be broadly divided into three main types, depending on the nature of the learning process and the kind of data provided. These are **Supervised Learning**, **Unsupervised Learning**, and **Reinforcement Learning**.

1. Supervised Learning

Supervised learning is the most common type of machine learning. In this method, the algorithm is trained on a labeled dataset, which means that the input data is paired with the correct output. The system "learns" by comparing its predictions with the actual outcomes and adjusts its model to improve accuracy over time.

Think of supervised learning like teaching a student with a set of flashcards. You show them a card with an image of an animal (input) and tell them that it's a cat (output). The student learns by memorizing these relationships, and over time, they get better at identifying cats when they see new images.

How it Works:

1. The system is given **input-output pairs** (e.g., an image of a dog labeled as "dog").
2. It processes this data and **learns** how to map inputs to the correct outputs.
3. The system then tries to **predict the output** for new, unseen data (e.g., an image of a new dog).
4. If the prediction is wrong, the system adjusts its internal model to be more accurate next time.

Real-World Examples:

- **Email spam filters:** These systems are trained on labeled examples of spam and non-spam emails. They learn to recognize patterns in the content and sender information to filter out unwanted messages.
- **Speech recognition:** Systems like Siri or Google Assistant learn to recognize words and phrases by being trained on large datasets of labeled speech.

2. Unsupervised Learning

Unsupervised learning is a bit different. In this case, the algorithm is given a dataset without any labeled outputs. The goal of the system is to identify patterns or structures in the data on its own. This type of learning is particularly useful when you want to explore a dataset to find hidden patterns without having predefined categories.

Think of unsupervised learning like letting a child sort a pile of toys without telling them what the categories are. The child might group the toys by color, size, or type, but they aren't given any explicit instructions. They have to figure out how to categorize the toys based on the similarities they notice.

How it Works:

1. The system is given **unlabeled data** (e.g., a pile of images of animals without any labels).
2. It tries to **find patterns** in the data by grouping similar items together.
3. The algorithm **clusters or organizes the data** based on these patterns (e.g., grouping images that look similar together).

Real-World Examples:

- **Customer segmentation:** Businesses often use unsupervised learning to group customers based on purchasing behavior. This helps them tailor marketing strategies to different customer segments.

- **Anomaly detection:** Unsupervised learning is also used to detect unusual data points that don't fit the general pattern. This is useful in fields like fraud detection, where the system can identify outliers (e.g., unusual transactions that might indicate fraud).

3. Reinforcement Learning

Reinforcement learning is inspired by how humans and animals learn through trial and error. In this type of machine learning, the system learns by interacting with an environment and receiving feedback in the form of rewards or punishments. The goal is to maximize the total reward over time by making the best possible decisions.

Think of reinforcement learning like teaching a dog to perform tricks. You reward the dog with a treat every time it successfully sits on command and withhold the reward when it doesn't. Over time, the dog learns that sitting on command leads to a positive outcome (the treat), so it adjusts its behavior to earn more rewards.

How it Works:

1. The system takes an **action** in an environment (e.g., moving a piece in a game).

2. It receives **feedback** based on the outcome of that action (e.g., a reward for a good move or a penalty for a bad move).

3. The system **adjusts its strategy** to maximize the total reward over time (e.g., it learns which moves lead to winning the game).

Real-World Examples:

- **Self-driving cars:** Reinforcement learning is used to teach autonomous vehicles how to drive by rewarding the car when it successfully navigates obstacles and penalizing it when it makes mistakes.

- **Game playing:** AI systems like **AlphaGo** and **OpenAI's Dota 2 bot** learned to play complex games through reinforcement learning, eventually beating human world champions.

Key Real-World Example: How Netflix and YouTube Recommend Content

Let's dive into a practical example of how machine learning is used in a real-world application: content recommendation on platforms like **Netflix** and **YouTube**.

If you've ever used Netflix, you've probably noticed how it seems to know exactly what you'd like to watch next. This isn't magic—

it's machine learning at work. Both Netflix and YouTube use **recommendation algorithms** that analyze your viewing habits and predict what content you're most likely to enjoy. Let's break down how this works.

How the Recommendation Engine Works

1. Data Collection

When you watch a show or movie on Netflix or a video on YouTube, the platform collects data about your activity. This includes:

- What you watched
- How long you watched it
- Whether you rated it (thumbs up/down on YouTube, or star rating on Netflix)
- What you've searched for
- What you've clicked on but didn't finish watching

These platforms collect this data not just from you, but from millions of users around the world.

2. Pattern Recognition

The recommendation system uses machine learning algorithms to analyze this massive dataset. It looks for patterns in your behavior— such as genres you prefer, how often you watch, and what time of day you tend to watch certain content.

It also looks at the behavior of users who are similar to you. For example, if many users who watched the same shows you did also liked a particular new release, the system may recommend that new show to you.

3. Predicting Preferences

Based on these patterns, the algorithm predicts what you're likely to watch next. The system makes these predictions using a combination of:

- **Collaborative filtering**: This method looks at what similar users have enjoyed. If other users with similar viewing habits to yours liked a particular show, it's likely that you will, too.

- **Content-based filtering**: This method recommends content that is similar to things you've watched in the past. If you've watched several documentaries, the system might suggest another documentary, even if no other users have watched it.

4. Continuous Improvement

The more you use Netflix or YouTube, the better the recommendation system becomes. Every time you watch, skip, or rate content, the algorithm learns more about your preferences and fine-tunes its recommendations accordingly.

Machine learning is a powerful tool that enables machines to learn from data, recognize patterns, and make decisions with minimal human intervention. In this chapter, we explored the three main types of machine learning: supervised learning, unsupervised learning, and reinforcement learning. Each type plays a different role in training systems to make predictions and decisions based on the data they're provided.

We also saw a key real-world example in action: how Netflix and YouTube use machine learning algorithms to recommend content. These platforms demonstrate the power of machine learning in creating personalized user experiences by analyzing vast amounts of data and making accurate predictions about user preferences.

In the next chapters, we will dive deeper into the technical aspects of how these algorithms work and explore other real-world applications of machine learning across various industries. But for now, you've got a solid understanding of how machines learn and how machine learning is impacting your daily life.

CHAPTER 3: DATA IS THE NEW OIL: UNDERSTANDING DATA IN AI

One of the most commonly heard phrases in the modern tech world is that "**data is the new oil**." But what does that mean, particularly in the context of artificial intelligence (AI) and machine learning (ML)? Just as oil fueled the industrial revolution, data powers the AI revolution today. Machines rely on vast amounts of data to learn, adapt, and make intelligent decisions. In this chapter, we will explore the central role that data plays in AI, break down the different types of data, and examine how a company like Google uses data to create personalized search experiences for billions of users around the globe.

The Role of Data in Machine Learning

To truly understand how data drives AI, it's helpful to think of machine learning as a student, and data as the textbook. A machine learning system learns from data in much the same way a student learns from reading textbooks and practicing problems. The more data the system is exposed to, the better it becomes at making accurate predictions or decisions. In fact, the effectiveness of any AI or machine learning system is largely determined by the quality and quantity of the data it's trained on.

Data is the Foundation of Machine Learning

For a machine learning model to work, it needs to be fed a substantial amount of data. This data serves as the **input** for the model, allowing the algorithm to detect patterns, trends, and relationships. Once the machine has processed the data, it uses this information to make predictions, classify items, or generate recommendations.

Let's use an analogy: imagine you're trying to teach a child to recognize different breeds of dogs. If you only show them a few pictures of dogs, their understanding will be limited. But if you show them hundreds or thousands of dog images, featuring different breeds, sizes, and angles, the child's ability to identify various dog breeds improves drastically. Similarly, machine learning models need large and diverse datasets to perform effectively.

Why More Data Improves Performance

One of the key strengths of machine learning is its ability to improve as more data becomes available. This concept is known as **scalability**—the ability of a system to handle increasing amounts of data without losing effectiveness. As the dataset grows, the machine learning model becomes more accurate and can make better decisions.

For example, in **spam email detection**, a model might initially be trained on 10,000 labeled emails—half of which are spam, and half of which are not. While this model could work reasonably well, its accuracy would improve if it were trained on 100,000 or even 1 million emails. With more examples, the model can better recognize subtle differences between legitimate and spam emails, refining its ability to classify future emails correctly.

However, the value of data is not just in its quantity—it's also about quality. Poor-quality data (e.g., data that is incomplete, inconsistent, or irrelevant) can lead to flawed models, a problem commonly referred to as **garbage in, garbage out**. This is why companies invest heavily in ensuring their data is clean, structured, and relevant to the problem at hand.

Structured vs. Unstructured Data

Not all data is created equal. In AI and machine learning, we typically categorize data into two main types: **structured data** and **unstructured data**. Understanding the difference between these two is key to appreciating how AI systems process information and make sense of the world.

Structured Data

Structured data refers to data that is organized in a clear and defined format, often stored in databases and spreadsheets. Structured data is neatly arranged into rows and columns, making it easy to search, sort, and analyze.

Examples of structured data include:

- **Customer information** in a database (names, addresses, phone numbers)
- **Sales data** such as the number of products sold, price, and date of sale
- **Bank transactions** that record amounts, transaction dates, and account numbers

This type of data is highly organized, often numerical, and easily processed by machine learning algorithms. Structured data fits neatly into **relational databases**, where each entry has a well-defined structure that makes querying and analysis straightforward.

Real-World Use of Structured Data

Consider an e-commerce platform like **Amazon**. Amazon tracks structured data about millions of transactions, including what items were purchased, how much they cost, and who bought them. By analyzing this structured data, Amazon can identify trends (e.g., which products are popular during specific times of year), optimize its supply chain, and make personalized product recommendations based on past purchase behavior.

Unstructured Data

Unstructured data, on the other hand, is data that does not follow a predefined format. It includes a vast range of data types, such as images, videos, social media posts, and text documents. Unstructured data is far more complex and harder to organize because it doesn't fit into neat rows and columns.

Examples of unstructured data include:

- **Emails** or customer reviews
- **Images** and **videos**
- **Social media posts**, blogs, and comments
- **Audio recordings** (like voice messages or podcasts)

Unstructured data is much harder to process and analyze because it lacks the organization of structured data. However, unstructured data often contains incredibly valuable insights. For example, sentiment analysis on unstructured social media posts can reveal how customers feel about a product or service in real time.

Real-World Use of Unstructured Data

Platforms like **Facebook** and **YouTube** deal with enormous volumes of unstructured data. Facebook processes billions of posts, images, and comments, while YouTube deals with countless hours of video uploaded every day. To make sense of this unstructured data, these companies use **deep learning** models, particularly neural networks, which excel at recognizing patterns in complex data types like images, audio, and text.

One prominent use case of unstructured data is in **facial recognition**. Systems like those used by Facebook's photo-tagging feature analyze unstructured data (i.e., user-uploaded photos) and use machine learning to identify faces and suggest tags for people in the image.

Real-World Example: Google Search and Data-Driven Personalization

One of the most powerful examples of AI and machine learning in action is **Google Search**. Every time you type a query into Google, an incredibly sophisticated system works behind the scenes to deliver the most relevant and personalized results possible. Google's ability to deliver precise search results stems from its vast use of data and machine learning algorithms.

How Google Search Uses Data

Google Search processes over **3.5 billion searches per day**, each contributing to a massive repository of search data. This data helps Google improve its search algorithms continuously, ensuring that results are increasingly accurate and relevant. There are several key ways in which data powers Google Search:

1. **Indexing   the   Web**
   Google uses web crawlers (also called spiders) to continuously browse the internet and collect data from websites. This information is stored in Google's index, which is like a giant database of all the content on the web. When you search for something, Google's algorithms quickly sift through this index to find relevant content.

2. **Understanding   User   Intent**
   Machine learning allows Google to understand the intent behind your search, even if you don't phrase it perfectly. For instance, if you search for "best laptop for programming," Google knows that you're looking for laptops suited for

programming, even if you didn't specify particular models or specs.

Google can do this because it has been trained on billions of past searches. It can recognize patterns in how users formulate their queries and which results they click on, allowing the algorithm to predict what kind of information will satisfy your query.

3. **Personalized Search Results**
Personalization is one of Google's most powerful features, and it's driven by the data it collects about individual users. Google tailors search results based on factors like your search history, location, and behavior on other Google services like YouTube or Gmail.

For example, if you frequently search for tech-related topics, Google will prioritize technology websites in your future searches. If you're searching for restaurants, Google will use your location to show nearby dining options. The more you use Google, the more personalized and relevant your search results become.

4. **Natural Language Processing (NLP)**
Google also employs **natural language processing** to understand the nuances of language. When you ask a question like, "What's the weather like in New York today?" Google uses NLP to understand that "weather" refers to a forecast and "New York today" refers to your location and

the current date. This allows Google to retrieve the most relevant, up-to-date information.

Machine Learning Behind the Scenes

Google uses a variety of machine learning techniques to improve the accuracy and efficiency of its search algorithms. One of the most important developments in recent years is the introduction of **RankBrain**, a machine learning system that helps Google interpret complex search queries.

What is RankBrain?

RankBrain is part of Google's overall search algorithm and is designed to handle ambiguous or unique queries—those that Google has never seen before. When you search for something highly specific or phrased in an unusual way, RankBrain helps the system understand the context and deliver relevant results.

For example, if you type in "What was the name of the tallest building in the world in 1990?", RankBrain analyzes your query and understands that you're looking for information about the Burj Khalifa (which wasn't completed until 2010). Even if the exact phrase doesn't appear in a web page, RankBrain's machine learning capabilities allow it to infer connections and deliver accurate information.

Data-Driven Personalization in Google Search

The data Google collects from your search habits not only enhances your experience but also allows Google to learn and improve its systems. Every time you search and click on a result, Google tracks this data to fine-tune future search rankings. If users frequently click on a particular link for a specific query, that page is likely relevant and may appear higher in future searches.

Additionally, Google tailors search results based on location and personal preferences. For example:

- If you're in London and search for "best coffee shop," Google will prioritize results for cafes near you.
- If you've previously shown interest in tech news by clicking on stories about the latest gadgets, Google may suggest more tech-related news in the future.

All of this is possible due to the vast amounts of data Google has collected over years of serving billions of users. Each search helps the system learn and adapt, providing more accurate and personalized results for future queries.

Conclusion

Data truly is the new oil in the age of AI and machine learning. Without it, even the most advanced algorithms would be ineffective. As we've seen, data serves as the foundation of machine learning systems, enabling them to learn, adapt, and improve over time.

Whether structured or unstructured, data is a critical resource that fuels AI's ability to understand and respond to the world.

We also explored how data-driven systems like Google Search use vast amounts of information to personalize and refine their services. Through powerful machine learning algorithms, Google can interpret user intent, deliver precise search results, and continuously improve its search capabilities.

In the next chapters, we will dive deeper into specific AI techniques and further explore how companies across industries are leveraging data to create intelligent systems that enhance everything from healthcare to entertainment.

CHAPTER 4: ALGORITHMS EXPLAINED: THE BRAINS BEHIND AI

At the heart of every artificial intelligence (AI) system is a set of instructions known as an **algorithm**. Algorithms are what make AI smart. They're the "brains" behind the technology, enabling machines to process data, make decisions, and learn from experience. In this chapter, we'll break down what algorithms are in simple terms, explore two popular types of algorithms—**Decision Trees** and **Neural Networks**—and take a real-world look at how algorithms power self-driving cars.

Simplified Explanation of Algorithms

In the simplest terms, an **algorithm** is a step-by-step set of rules or instructions that a computer follows to solve a specific problem. Just as a chef follows a recipe to bake a cake, an algorithm provides a sequence of instructions for a machine to perform a task.

Let's think of an everyday example: If you were to create an algorithm to sort a stack of books by title, you might follow these steps:

1. Pick up the first book in the stack.
2. Compare its title to the next book in the stack.

3. If the first book comes before the second alphabetically, keep the order. If not, swap them.
4. Repeat this process for every pair of books until the entire stack is sorted alphabetically.

This is a basic sorting algorithm. In AI and machine learning, algorithms are more complex, but they follow the same basic principle: they take input data, process it according to a set of rules, and produce an output or decision.

How Algorithms Work in AI

In AI, algorithms drive the process of learning and decision-making. They analyze data, detect patterns, and use those patterns to make predictions or decisions. For example, when you get a recommendation from Netflix or YouTube, it's because an algorithm has analyzed your past viewing habits and identified patterns that suggest what you might want to watch next.

Machine learning algorithms, in particular, improve over time as they are exposed to more data. They adjust their internal parameters to better reflect the patterns in the data, gradually improving their performance.

In simple terms: **An algorithm is a set of instructions that tells a machine how to solve a problem or make a decision. In AI, these instructions allow the machine to learn from data and improve its decision-making over time.**

Examples of Popular Algorithms: Decision Trees and Neural Networks

AI is powered by a wide range of algorithms, each suited to different kinds of problems. Let's explore two of the most commonly used types of algorithms in AI: **Decision Trees** and **Neural Networks**. These are foundational algorithms that power many AI systems, from recommendation engines to facial recognition technologies.

1. Decision Trees

A **Decision Tree** is a simple yet powerful algorithm that mimics the process of human decision-making. It works by splitting data into branches based on certain conditions, creating a tree-like structure that leads to a final decision. Each "branch" represents a possible outcome of a decision, and the process continues until the algorithm reaches a decision, which is represented by a "leaf" at the end of the branch.

How Decision Trees Work

Imagine you're trying to decide which movie to watch, and you have a simple decision-making process:

1. **Step 1:** Do you want to watch a comedy? (Yes/No)
2. **Step 2:** If yes, do you prefer classic or modern comedies?
3. **Step 3:** If no, do you want to watch an action movie or a drama?

Each question narrows down your choices until you arrive at a decision. In this example, the algorithm asks a series of questions (like branches) to sort through the possibilities and reach a decision (the leaf).

Example of a Decision Tree in AI

In machine learning, decision trees are often used for **classification tasks**, where the goal is to assign data to different categories. For example, in a medical diagnosis system, a decision tree might be used to determine whether a patient has a certain disease based on symptoms and test results. The algorithm would ask questions like, "Does the patient have a fever?" and "Is the white blood cell count elevated?" Each answer would guide the algorithm down a different branch until it reaches a final diagnosis.

Strengths and Weaknesses

- **Strengths:** Decision trees are easy to understand and interpret, making them useful for explaining decisions. They also work well with both categorical and numerical data.
- **Weaknesses:** Decision trees can become overly complex and "overfit" the data, meaning they may perform well on the training data but poorly on new, unseen data.

2. Neural Networks

If decision trees are like a flowchart, **Neural Networks** are more like the human brain. Neural networks are a class of machine learning algorithms inspired by how the brain's neurons work. They are particularly powerful for tasks like image recognition, speech processing, and natural language understanding.

How Neural Networks Work

A neural network consists of layers of **nodes** (also called neurons), which are interconnected. The simplest neural network has three types of layers:

1. **Input layer**: This is where the raw data enters the network (e.g., an image or a string of text).
2. **Hidden layers**: These layers process the data by performing mathematical calculations. There can be multiple hidden layers, which is why deep neural networks are often referred to as "deep learning."
3. **Output layer**: This layer provides the final decision or prediction (e.g., identifying whether an image contains a cat or a dog).

Each connection between nodes has a weight, which adjusts as the network learns. When data is passed through the network, these weights help the network decide how much emphasis to place on certain features of the data. Over time, the network "learns" which patterns are important and becomes better at making accurate predictions.

Example of a Neural Network in AI

Neural networks are widely used in **image recognition** tasks. For example, when Facebook automatically tags you in photos, it uses a neural network to analyze the image and identify faces. The neural network processes the pixels of the image, learns what features make up a human face (like the shape of eyes, nose, and mouth), and then matches those features to known faces in its database.

Strengths and Weaknesses

- **Strengths:** Neural networks are incredibly powerful and flexible, capable of handling complex tasks that involve unstructured data like images, videos, and natural language.
- **Weaknesses:** Neural networks require large amounts of data and computational power to be effective. They can also be difficult to interpret, as the decision-making process inside the network can be opaque (often referred to as the "black box" problem).

Real-World Example: Self-Driving Cars and the Decision-Making Process

One of the most fascinating and complex applications of AI algorithms is in **self-driving cars**. Companies like Tesla, Waymo, and Uber are using AI to develop autonomous vehicles that can navigate roads, make decisions, and avoid obstacles—all without human intervention. Let's explore how algorithms like decision trees and neural networks help self-driving cars make real-time decisions.

How Self-Driving Cars Use Algorithms

Self-driving cars rely on a combination of sensors, cameras, radar, and AI algorithms to understand their environment and make driving decisions. These algorithms process data from the car's surroundings (e.g., other vehicles, pedestrians, traffic signs) and determine the best course of action.

Step 1: Perception

The first step in autonomous driving is **perception**, where the car uses sensors and cameras to gather data about its surroundings. Neural networks play a crucial role in this stage, helping the car "see" and interpret objects around it. For example, a neural network processes the images captured by the car's cameras to detect traffic signs, lane markings, and other vehicles.

Neural networks are especially good at **object recognition**, which is critical for self-driving cars. The car needs to differentiate between a pedestrian, a cyclist, and another vehicle, and it relies on the neural network to classify these objects accurately.

Step 2: Decision-Making

Once the car has perceived its environment, it must make decisions about how to navigate. This is where decision trees and other algorithms come into play. The car's decision-making process involves choosing the best action based on multiple factors, such as the car's speed, the distance to the next vehicle, and the current road conditions.

Imagine the car is approaching an intersection. It must decide whether to:

- Stop at a red light.
- Slow down for a pedestrian crossing.
- Turn left if there's no oncoming traffic.

In this case, a **decision tree algorithm** could help the car make the right choice by asking a series of yes/no questions:

1. Is the traffic light red?
2. Is there a pedestrian crossing the street?
3. Is there enough space to turn left?

The car's decision tree evaluates these factors and selects the safest action.

Step 3: Motion Planning and Control

Finally, once the car has made a decision, it needs to execute that decision smoothly and safely. **Motion planning algorithms** determine the exact path the car should take, considering factors like speed, road curvature, and potential obstacles. These algorithms continuously adjust the car's movements to ensure a safe and comfortable ride.

For example, if the car decides to turn left, the motion planning algorithm calculates the ideal speed and trajectory to make the turn without hitting other vehicles or pedestrians. This requires real-time adjustments as new data comes in from the car's sensors.

The Role of Data in Self-Driving Cars

Just like in other AI applications, self-driving cars rely heavily on data. The car continuously collects data from its sensors, processes that data with AI algorithms, and uses it to make driving decisions. Over time, these cars learn from their experiences on the road, improving their performance with each drive.

For instance, if the car encounters a new type of obstacle (like a construction zone), it uses the data from that experience to update its decision-making process. In the future, when the car encounters a similar situation, it will know how to handle it more effectively.

Conclusion

Algorithms are the essential building blocks that power AI systems, enabling machines to process data, make decisions, and learn over time. In this chapter, we explored the basics of algorithms and delved into two popular types—**Decision Trees** and **Neural Networks**—that play a crucial role in many AI applications. We also examined how these algorithms are used in the real world, particularly in the development of self-driving cars.

Whether it's recognizing objects in an image, predicting the next movie you'll watch, or making split-second driving decisions, algorithms are the key to unlocking AI's full potential. As we continue to explore the world of AI, understanding how these algorithms work will deepen your appreciation for the power and complexity of modern AI systems.

In the next chapters, we'll dive deeper into the specific applications of AI across various industries, from healthcare to finance, and explore how different algorithms are being used to solve some of the world's most challenging problems.

CHAPTER 5: AI IN EVERYDAY LIFE: SMARTPHONES, SMART HOMES, AND MORE

Artificial intelligence (AI) isn't just powering industrial robots or self-driving cars—it's deeply embedded in our daily lives, often in ways we don't even realize. From the smartphones we rely on to smart home devices that control our living spaces, AI is seamlessly integrated into the tools we use every day. In this chapter, we'll explore how AI is the invisible force behind virtual assistants like Siri and Alexa, smart home devices like thermostats and security systems, and even the simple convenience of predictive text in messaging apps.

How AI Powers Everyday Tools: Siri, Alexa, and Google Assistant

Virtual assistants like **Apple's Siri**, **Amazon's Alexa**, and **Google Assistant** are prime examples of AI in action, simplifying daily tasks and creating a more personalized digital experience. These voice-activated assistants harness a range of AI technologies, including **natural language processing (NLP)** and **machine learning**, to understand and respond to user commands.

Natural Language Processing (NLP) in Virtual Assistants

One of the key components of virtual assistants is **natural language processing (NLP)**, which allows machines to understand, interpret, and respond to human language. When you ask Siri, "What's the weather like today?" or tell Alexa to "play some jazz," the system uses NLP to:

1. **Recognize the command**: The AI translates your spoken words into text.
2. **Understand the intent**: It processes the meaning behind your words. Are you asking for information, or giving a command?
3. **Generate a response**: Based on the intent, the system searches its database for the most appropriate response, such as displaying the weather forecast or playing a music playlist.

This process might seem simple, but it involves sophisticated algorithms that must handle the complexities of language, such as different accents, speech patterns, and even nuances like sarcasm or humor.

Example: Siri's Functionality

Apple's **Siri**, for example, goes beyond simple voice commands. Over time, Siri learns from your behavior to provide more personalized responses. If you regularly call a particular person on your way home from work, Siri may start suggesting you make that call as soon as you leave your office. It can also access apps, manage calendar events, set reminders, and even control smart home devices, all by processing spoken language.

Example: Alexa and Google Assistant in Smart Homes

Similarly, **Amazon's Alexa** and **Google Assistant** are integrated into smart home ecosystems, allowing you to control everything from lights to thermostats with voice commands. You might say, "Alexa, turn on the living room lights," and the system will relay the command to your connected devices, adjusting the lights accordingly.

These assistants also benefit from **machine learning**, which enables them to improve their responses over time. Every interaction you have with a virtual assistant is logged, analyzed, and used to refine future interactions. This is why Alexa or Google Assistant might be more accurate in understanding your commands after a few weeks of regular use—they're constantly learning and improving.

AI in Smart Home Devices: Thermostats, Lights, and Security Systems

As AI becomes more embedded in our homes, it is transforming how we interact with our living spaces. **Smart home devices** powered by AI offer convenience, efficiency, and increased control over various aspects of our daily environment. These devices use sensors, data analysis, and machine learning to automate tasks, respond to changes in your preferences, and enhance security.

Smart Thermostats

One of the most popular smart home devices is the **smart thermostat**, with the **Nest Thermostat** being a prime example. Smart thermostats use AI to learn your daily routines and adjust the temperature in your home accordingly.

How It Works:

1. **Learning from your behavior**: When you adjust the temperature manually, the thermostat remembers these settings. Over time, it learns your preferences— such as lowering the temperature at night or heating the house before you wake up in the morning.

2. **Automated adjustments**: After observing your routine, the thermostat can make automatic adjustments, like turning off the heating when you leave the house and warming it up just before you return.

3. **Energy savings**: By optimizing the heating and cooling schedule, smart thermostats can help reduce energy usage, potentially saving on utility bills. Many smart thermostats even provide energy usage reports, offering insights into how much energy is being used and when.

This ability to learn and adapt is powered by machine learning algorithms that process data about your habits, local weather conditions, and even energy consumption trends to optimize the temperature in your home.

Smart Lights

Smart lighting systems are another common AI-driven innovation in the home. Systems like **Philips Hue** use AI to provide personalized lighting experiences, and can be controlled remotely via apps or voice commands through virtual assistants like Alexa or Google Assistant.

Features of Smart Lights:

- **Voice control**: You can tell your assistant, "Turn off the bedroom lights," or even create custom scenes like "Movie Night" to dim the lights to a specific level.
- **Automated schedules**: Smart lights can be set to turn on or off at specific times or adjust their brightness based on the time of day. For example, they can automatically brighten in the morning to help wake you up or dim in the evening for relaxation.
- **Energy efficiency**: Similar to smart thermostats, smart lighting systems can help reduce energy consumption by turning off when not needed, based on sensors or your habits.

Smart Security Systems

Smart security systems have also seen a significant boost from AI technology, particularly in the areas of facial recognition and real-time monitoring. Companies like **Ring** and **Nest** provide security cameras, doorbell cameras, and alarm systems that use AI to enhance home security.

How AI Enhances Security:

1. **Facial recognition**: Some advanced security systems are equipped with facial recognition technology. The AI can distinguish between familiar faces (e.g., family members) and unknown individuals. This helps reduce false alarms and improves overall security.

2. **Real-time monitoring and alerts**: AI algorithms analyze video feeds from security cameras in real time, detecting unusual movements or activity. If the system spots something out of the ordinary, it can send an alert to your smartphone, allowing you to check the live feed and take action if necessary.

3. **Smart locks**: AI-powered smart locks allow you to lock or unlock doors remotely, set up temporary access for guests, or automatically lock the door when you leave.

These smart home devices demonstrate how AI can take simple, everyday tasks—like adjusting the temperature or turning off the lights—and make them more convenient, efficient, and secure. As smart homes continue to evolve, AI will play an even larger role in automating and enhancing daily life.

Real-World Example: Predictive Text and Autocorrect in Messaging Apps

Another familiar example of AI in everyday life is **predictive text** and **autocorrect** in messaging apps. Whether you're typing a message in WhatsApp, composing an email, or sending a text on your smartphone, AI is working in the background to make communication faster and more accurate.

How Predictive Text Works

Predictive text is a feature that suggests words or phrases based on what you've already typed, helping you compose messages more quickly. This feature is powered by AI algorithms that analyze patterns in your typing behavior, as well as broader language usage trends.

The Process:

1. **Analyzing context**: As you type, the algorithm predicts the next word or phrase you're likely to use based on the current context. For example, if you start typing,

"See you," the system might suggest "later" or "soon" as the next word.

2. **Learning from your behavior**: Over time, predictive text becomes more personalized, learning your unique writing style, common phrases, and even frequently used slang or emojis. This is why your phone might suggest specific words that you use regularly but wouldn't show to someone else.

3. **Adapting to language changes**: The system continuously updates its language model based on new data, meaning it can adapt to evolving language trends, including slang, abbreviations, or newly popular terms.

Machine learning plays a significant role in improving predictive text over time. Every time you accept or reject a suggestion, the system learns from your choice and refines its predictions for future messages.

How Autocorrect Works

Similarly, **autocorrect** uses AI to improve the accuracy of your typing by automatically correcting typos or misspelled words. While predictive text suggests words before you've typed them, autocorrect steps in after you've typed, correcting mistakes in real-time.

The Process:

1. **Detecting typos**: When you make a typo, the autocorrect system compares the misspelled word to its internal dictionary of correctly spelled words.

2. **Contextual correction**: Autocorrect doesn't just replace a misspelled word with the closest match; it considers the context of the entire sentence to choose the most appropriate correction. For example, if you type "I'll meet you their," autocorrect knows "their" should be replaced with "there" based on the sentence structure.

3. **Learning your preferences**: Just like predictive text, autocorrect improves as it learns from your typing habits. It remembers words you frequently use that might not be in its default dictionary—such as names, slang, or technical terms—and avoids correcting them in the future.

AI in Action: Google's Smart Compose

A more advanced version of predictive text is **Google's Smart Compose** feature in Gmail. Smart Compose not only predicts individual words but also suggests entire phrases or sentences as you type. For example, if you start typing an email with "I hope you're doing well," Smart Compose might suggest the next sentence, "Let me know if you have any questions."

Smart Compose is powered by **deep learning**, a branch of AI that uses neural networks to understand language patterns. This system has been trained on vast amounts of email data, allowing it to recognize common email structures and provide useful suggestions that save time and reduce typing effort.

Conclusion to Chapter 5

AI has woven itself into the fabric of our daily lives, often in ways that feel almost invisible. From virtual assistants like Siri and Alexa that respond to voice commands to smart home devices that adjust our environment automatically, AI is transforming how we interact with technology. Even something as simple as predictive text and autocorrect in messaging apps demonstrates the incredible power of AI to make our lives easier, more efficient, and more connected.

As AI continues to evolve, we can expect even more seamless integration of intelligent systems into the devices and tools we use every day. Whether it's learning from our behavior to offer personalized recommendations or automating routine tasks, AI is fundamentally changing the way we live, work, and communicate.

CHAPTER 6: NATURAL LANGUAGE PROCESSING (NLP): HOW MACHINES UNDERSTAND LANGUAGE

Language is the primary way humans communicate, share ideas, and express emotions. But what happens when machines need to understand and process human language? This is where **Natural Language Processing (NLP)** comes into play. NLP is a field of artificial intelligence that enables machines to understand, interpret, and respond to human language in a meaningful way. In this chapter, we'll explore what NLP is, why it's important, and how it's applied in everyday tools like Google Translate and chatbots. We'll also dive into a real-world example of how sentiment analysis, a core application of NLP, is transforming customer service.

What is Natural Language Processing (NLP), and Why is it Important?

Natural Language Processing (NLP) is a branch of AI that focuses on the interaction between computers and humans through natural language. It combines aspects of linguistics, computer science, and machine learning to enable machines to process and understand language just like a human would. Essentially, NLP is what allows machines to read, interpret, and respond to text or spoken words.

The Complexity of Human Language

Human language is inherently complex. We use slang, idiomatic expressions, sarcasm, and ambiguous phrases, which make it difficult for machines to fully grasp meaning. Moreover, language varies across cultures, regions, and contexts, adding another layer of complexity to NLP.

For example:

- The word "bank" can refer to a financial institution or the edge of a river. Determining the correct meaning depends on the context of the sentence.
- A phrase like "It's raining cats and dogs" is understood by humans as heavy rain, but without context or cultural knowledge, a machine might interpret it literally.

NLP is important because it allows AI to handle these complexities, making it possible for machines to interact with humans in a natural, intuitive way. From virtual assistants to real-time translations, NLP bridges the gap between human communication and machine intelligence.

Why is NLP Important?

NLP plays a critical role in making AI applications more useful and accessible to everyday users. It allows machines to understand and process the vast amount of unstructured data found in written or spoken language, which accounts for a significant portion of the information available online. This makes NLP essential for:

- **Search engines**: Understanding user queries and delivering accurate search results.
- **Virtual assistants**: Processing spoken commands and responding appropriately.
- **Translation tools**: Converting text from one language to another with contextual accuracy.
- **Content moderation**: Detecting inappropriate content or hate speech on social media platforms.

In short, NLP is the technology that makes it possible for AI to interact with humans using language, rather than requiring users to interact through complex programming or coding languages.

Real-World Applications: Google Translate, Chatbots, and Text Analysis

NLP is embedded in many of the tools we use every day. It powers everything from machine translation services to chatbots that handle customer service inquiries. Let's take a closer look at some of the most widespread real-world applications of NLP.

Google Translate: Breaking Language Barriers with NLP

One of the most famous applications of NLP is **Google Translate**, a machine translation service that enables users to translate text or speech from one language to another in real time. Google Translate relies on NLP to interpret the meaning of the input text, translate it, and ensure the translation is as accurate as possible given the context.

How Google Translate Works

Google Translate uses **neural machine translation (NMT)**, a type of deep learning model that processes entire sentences as a whole rather than translating word by word. This helps the system better understand the meaning of a sentence and generate more accurate translations by taking context into account.

For example, translating the sentence "He's cool" into French can have different meanings based on context. Is "cool" referring to someone's temperament (calm) or their popularity (hip)? NMT models process the entire sentence to determine the most appropriate translation.

Over time, Google Translate has improved its ability to handle idiomatic expressions, slang, and phrases that don't have direct equivalents in other languages. This is made possible by analyzing vast datasets of multilingual text and applying machine learning to improve its models.

Chatbots: Automating Conversations with NLP

Chatbots are another prominent application of NLP. From customer service agents to virtual shopping assistants, chatbots are designed to simulate conversation with human users. They use NLP to understand user input, respond appropriately, and carry out tasks like answering questions, making reservations, or offering technical support.

How Chatbots Use NLP

When a user interacts with a chatbot, NLP enables the system to:

1. **Interpret the user's message**: The chatbot processes the input using **natural language understanding (NLU)**, which allows it to extract the meaning and intent behind the words. For example, when a user says, "I need help with my order," the chatbot understands that the user is seeking support for an order issue.

2. **Generate a response**: After understanding the intent, the chatbot uses **natural language generation (NLG)** to craft a response. If the user is asking for order details, the chatbot might respond with, "Can you please provide your order number?"

3. **Carry out tasks**: Many chatbots are integrated with backend systems, allowing them to carry out actions such as tracking shipments, booking appointments, or resolving issues without human intervention.

Chatbots are widely used in industries like e-commerce, healthcare, and banking. Companies use chatbots to handle high volumes of customer inquiries quickly and efficiently, offering 24/7 service with minimal human input.

Text Analysis: Extracting Meaning from Unstructured Data

One of the most powerful applications of NLP is **text analysis**, which involves processing large amounts of unstructured text data to extract meaningful insights. Businesses, government agencies, and researchers use text analysis tools to understand trends, analyze sentiment, and monitor social media for brand mentions or public sentiment.

Example: Social Media Monitoring

Social media platforms generate massive amounts of unstructured data in the form of tweets, posts, comments, and reviews. NLP is used to monitor this data and extract valuable insights, such as:

- Identifying trending topics or emerging themes.
- Detecting public sentiment about a brand, product, or event.
- Monitoring for inappropriate content or hate speech.

Tools like **Sprout Social** and **Hootsuite** use NLP-powered text analysis to help companies manage their social media presence and track user sentiment in real time. By analyzing keywords, hashtags, and user interactions, these tools allow businesses to gauge the success of marketing campaigns, respond to customer feedback, and stay ahead of public opinion.

Example: Sentiment Analysis in Customer Service

One specific application of NLP that has gained significant traction in recent years is **sentiment analysis**, a technique used to determine the emotional tone behind a body of text. This can be particularly useful in customer service, where understanding how customers feel about a product, service, or experience is critical to maintaining satisfaction and loyalty.

What is Sentiment Analysis?

Sentiment analysis is the process of using NLP algorithms to classify a piece of text as positive, negative, or neutral. It helps businesses understand the emotional undertone of customer feedback, such as reviews, social media posts, or emails. Sentiment analysis can be applied to any text where it's important to detect subjective opinions or attitudes.

For instance, a customer review saying, "The product works great, and the service was fantastic!" would be classified as positive sentiment, while a comment like, "I'm disappointed with how long the delivery took," would be categorized as negative sentiment.

How Sentiment Analysis Works

Sentiment analysis uses a combination of **machine learning** and **lexical analysis** to understand the polarity (positive, negative, or neutral) of text. Here's how it works:

1. **Text preprocessing**: The text is first cleaned and standardized. This includes removing stopwords (common words like "and" or "the" that don't add meaning), converting all text to lowercase, and

tokenizing (breaking the text into smaller units like words or phrases).

2. **Feature extraction**: The system identifies key features in the text, such as sentiment-laden words (e.g., "love," "hate," "amazing," "terrible") and context-specific terms that may influence the sentiment.

3. **Sentiment classification**: Using a trained model, the system classifies the text as positive, negative, or neutral based on the identified features.

Real-World Application: Sentiment Analysis in Customer Service

In the realm of customer service, sentiment analysis is widely used to monitor customer feedback across different channels—such as emails, chat logs, reviews, and social media. Companies like **Amazon**, **Delta Airlines**, and **Zappos** use sentiment analysis to quickly identify customer dissatisfaction and address it before it escalates.

Benefits for Businesses:

*   **Detecting customer frustration early**: If a sentiment analysis tool detects a spike in negative feedback (e.g., many customers complaining about shipping delays or defective products), customer service teams can proactively address the issue.

- **Prioritizing responses**: Sentiment analysis can help prioritize customer inquiries based on urgency. For example, a customer whose message is classified as "very negative" might be given higher priority in the response queue.

- **Improving products and services**: By analyzing the sentiment behind customer reviews, companies can identify areas where products or services need improvement. For instance, if many reviews mention poor battery life, the company can focus on improving that aspect in future updates

Example: Delta Airlines and Sentiment Monitoring

Delta Airlines uses sentiment analysis to monitor tweets and social media posts from its customers. When a customer posts a negative comment about a delayed flight or poor service, Delta's system flags the post, and customer service agents can respond quickly to resolve the issue. This real-time sentiment tracking allows the airline to address problems before they escalate, improving customer satisfaction and potentially preventing public relations issues.

Conclusion

Natural Language Processing (NLP) is one of the most transformative technologies in AI, enabling machines to understand and interact with human language in a meaningful way. From the translation services of **Google Translate** to the customer service capabilities of **chatbots**, NLP plays a vital role in creating smarter, more intuitive AI systems that can engage with users on their own terms.

We've also seen how **sentiment analysis** is being used in real-world applications like customer service, allowing businesses to monitor feedback, detect dissatisfaction, and improve their interactions with customers. As NLP continues to advance, we can expect even more sophisticated tools that understand not only the words we say but also the deeper context and emotions behind them.

In the next chapter, we'll explore how AI is revolutionizing the healthcare industry, from diagnostics to drug discovery, and how NLP is helping doctors and researchers make sense of vast amounts of medical data.

CHAPTER 7: AI IN HEALTHCARE: FROM DIAGNOSTICS TO DRUG DISCOVERY

Artificial intelligence (AI) is revolutionizing healthcare by improving patient outcomes, streamlining clinical workflows, and accelerating medical research. From diagnostics to drug discovery, AI's ability to analyze vast amounts of data and generate meaningful insights is transforming the way we approach healthcare. In this chapter, we will explore how AI is being applied in the medical field, look at real-world examples like **IBM Watson** in cancer diagnosis and AI-driven drug discovery, and discuss the potential future of AI in personalized medicine.

How AI is Transforming Healthcare

Healthcare has long been driven by data, whether it's patient medical records, lab results, or clinical research findings. However, the sheer volume and complexity of this data make it difficult for human doctors and researchers to process and analyze it all. This is where AI comes in. AI algorithms, particularly those based on **machine learning** and **deep learning**, excel at processing large datasets, identifying patterns, and making predictions based on those patterns.

Here's how AI is transforming healthcare:

1. Enhanced Diagnostics

One of AI's most promising applications is in medical diagnostics. AI algorithms can analyze medical images, scans, and other diagnostic data to detect abnormalities and help doctors make faster, more accurate diagnoses. AI systems can be trained to recognize patterns in medical data that may be too subtle or complex for the human eye, improving early detection of diseases like cancer, heart disease, and neurological disorders.

For example, **AI-powered imaging systems** can analyze mammograms or CT scans to detect tumors at a much earlier stage than traditional methods. In ophthalmology, AI is used to examine retinal images to detect signs of diabetic retinopathy, a condition that can lead to blindness if untreated.

2. Predictive Analytics

AI is also transforming healthcare through predictive analytics, which can help healthcare providers anticipate patient outcomes, manage chronic diseases, and predict the spread of infectious diseases. By analyzing data from electronic health records (EHRs), genetic tests, and wearable devices, AI algorithms can identify patients at high risk of developing specific conditions, allowing for earlier interventions.

In hospitals, predictive analytics can help optimize operations by predicting patient admission rates, reducing wait times, and improving the allocation of medical resources. During public health crises, such as the COVID-19 pandemic, AI-driven predictive models have been used to forecast infection rates and guide policy decisions.

3. Streamlined Clinical Workflows

AI is being used to automate routine administrative tasks, allowing healthcare professionals to focus more on patient care. Natural language processing (NLP) algorithms are employed to transcribe doctors' notes, streamline medical billing, and manage patient records. By reducing the administrative burden on healthcare providers, AI enables faster, more efficient care.

4. Personalized Medicine

One of the most transformative promises of AI in healthcare is the development of personalized medicine, where treatment plans are tailored to the individual patient's genetic makeup, lifestyle, and medical history. AI can analyze genomic data to identify the best therapies for specific patients, reducing the trial-and-error approach that is often used in medicine today.

In the future, personalized medicine will become even more precise as AI continues to analyze complex data sets, leading to highly targeted treatments for diseases like cancer, diabetes, and autoimmune disorders.

Real-World Examples: IBM Watson in Cancer Diagnosis, AI for Drug Discovery

While the potential for AI in healthcare is vast, let's focus on two real-world examples where AI is already making a significant impact: **IBM Watson in cancer diagnosis** and **AI-powered drug discovery**.

IBM Watson in Cancer Diagnosis

IBM Watson Health is one of the most well-known applications of AI in healthcare. Watson is a cognitive computing system that uses machine learning and natural language processing to analyze vast amounts of medical data and assist doctors in diagnosing diseases, particularly cancer.

How IBM Watson Works

IBM Watson's cancer diagnosis tool, **Watson for Oncology**, works by analyzing patient medical records, clinical trial data, and medical literature to provide doctors with evidence-based treatment options. Watson can process millions of pages of medical research and match that information with a patient's unique case, including their genetic data, to recommend the most effective treatments.

For example, if a patient is diagnosed with breast cancer, Watson can analyze data from similar cases, consider the patient's genetic makeup, and suggest treatment options based on current medical guidelines and the latest research. This saves doctors time and ensures that patients receive the most up-to-date care.

Real-World Impact

In practice, IBM Watson has been used in hospitals around the world to assist oncologists in making more informed treatment decisions. A study conducted at the **Manipal Hospitals** in India showed that Watson's recommendations matched those of doctors in 96% of cases for breast cancer treatments. This demonstrates the potential of AI to provide decision support in complex medical cases, particularly when doctors are overwhelmed by the sheer volume of medical literature and patient data.

While Watson has seen success in many cases, there are challenges to fully integrating AI into routine healthcare practice. One of the primary challenges is ensuring that the AI system is trained on a diverse range of data to avoid biased or incomplete recommendations.

AI for Drug Discovery

The process of discovering and developing new drugs is typically long, costly, and risky. It can take over a decade and billions of dollars to bring a new drug to market. However, AI is now being used to significantly speed up this process, reduce costs, and identify potential treatments for diseases more efficiently.

How AI is Transforming Drug Discovery

AI-powered drug discovery platforms use machine learning algorithms to analyze vast datasets of chemical compounds, genetic information, and biological processes to predict which compounds are most likely to be effective in treating specific diseases. These systems can model how different drugs interact with proteins, cells, and genetic markers, allowing researchers to focus on the most promising candidates.

AI is particularly useful in identifying potential **drug repurposing** opportunities—finding new uses for existing drugs. During the COVID-19 pandemic, for example, AI algorithms were used to screen existing medications for potential effectiveness against the virus, helping accelerate the development of treatments.

Example: Benevolent AI and COVID-19

Benevolent AI, a British biotech company, uses AI to discover new treatments for diseases. During the COVID-19 pandemic, the company applied its AI platform to identify existing drugs that could potentially inhibit the virus's ability to replicate. Within weeks, Benevolent AI identified **baricitinib**, a drug originally developed to treat rheumatoid arthritis, as a candidate for treating COVID-19. Clinical trials confirmed the drug's efficacy, and it was subsequently repurposed for use in COVID-19 patients.

Example: Insilico Medicine

Another example is **Insilico Medicine**, which uses AI to discover new drugs. The company's AI platform can analyze biological data to generate new drug candidates in a matter of days. In 2020, Insilico's AI platform identified several potential drug candidates for **fibrosis**, a disease that leads to scarring of tissue. The discovery process took just 46 days, a fraction of the time it would have taken using traditional methods.

The Impact of AI on Drug Discovery

AI has the potential to significantly reduce the time and cost associated with drug development. By accelerating the discovery process and narrowing down potential candidates early on, AI can help bring life-saving treatments to patients faster. Moreover, AI-powered drug discovery can tackle diseases that have been difficult to treat using conventional methods, opening up new possibilities for medical breakthroughs.

The Future of AI in Personalized Medicine

One of the most exciting frontiers of AI in healthcare is its potential to revolutionize **personalized medicine**. Traditionally, healthcare has operated on a "one-size-fits-all" approach, where treatments are designed to work for the average patient. However, individual patients respond to treatments differently based on their unique genetic makeup, lifestyle, and environment.

AI has the potential to analyze these complex factors and develop highly personalized treatment plans tailored to the specific needs of each patient. Here's how AI is shaping the future of personalized medicine:

1. Genomic Medicine

AI is being used to analyze **genomic data** (a person's complete set of DNA) to identify genetic mutations or variations that may increase the risk of certain diseases, such as cancer, heart disease, or Alzheimer's. By understanding a patient's genetic profile, doctors can recommend targeted therapies that are more likely to be effective based on the individual's genetic makeup.

Example: AI and Cancer Treatment

In cancer treatment, AI can be used to analyze a patient's genetic mutations to identify the most effective drug therapies. Some cancers are driven by specific genetic mutations, and AI algorithms can rapidly analyze genomic data to match patients with the therapies most likely to target those mutations.

2. AI-Driven Biomarker Discovery

Biomarkers are measurable indicators of a biological condition or disease. AI can analyze vast amounts of biological data to identify new biomarkers that can predict disease progression or treatment response. This allows for earlier detection of diseases and more precise treatments.

Example: Alzheimer's Disease

Researchers are using AI to discover biomarkers for **Alzheimer's disease**. By analyzing brain scans and genetic data, AI systems can identify early signs of the disease long before symptoms appear, allowing for earlier interventions and potential treatments that could slow the progression of the disease.

3. Wearable Devices and Real-Time Monitoring

Wearable devices, such as fitness trackers and smartwatches, are increasingly equipped with AI-powered sensors that can monitor vital signs like heart rate, blood pressure, and glucose levels in real time. These devices generate continuous streams of data that can be analyzed by AI to detect anomalies, predict health issues, and recommend personalized interventions.

Example: Diabetes Management

For patients with diabetes, AI-powered wearable devices can monitor blood glucose levels throughout the day. By analyzing this data in real time, AI systems can predict when a patient's blood sugar is likely to spike or drop and suggest actions, such as taking insulin or adjusting their diet. This personalized approach helps patients manage their condition more effectively and prevent complications.

4. AI-Enhanced Clinical Trials

Clinical trials are essential for testing new treatments, but they are often time-consuming and expensive. AI can help streamline clinical trials by identifying the most suitable participants based on genetic profiles, medical histories, and other factors. This targeted recruitment process can lead to more efficient trials and faster approval of new therapies.

Example: AI in Oncology Trials

In oncology, AI is being used to match cancer patients with clinical trials that are most likely to benefit them based on their unique genetic mutations. This increases the likelihood of successful outcomes and speeds up the development of new cancer treatments.

Conclusion

AI is transforming healthcare in profound ways, from improving diagnostics and streamlining clinical workflows to accelerating drug discovery and paving the way for personalized medicine. Real-world examples like **IBM Watson** in cancer diagnosis and AI-driven drug discovery by companies like **BenevolentAI** and **Insilico Medicine** demonstrate the powerful impact AI is already having in the medical field.

As AI continues to evolve, the future of healthcare will be more personalized, precise, and efficient. Patients will benefit from treatments tailored to their genetic profiles, diseases will be detected and treated earlier, and new therapies will be developed faster than ever before. AI is not just enhancing healthcare—it is redefining what's possible in medicine.

In the next chapter, we'll explore how AI is transforming the financial industry, from fraud detection to personalized financial advice, and examine the ethical challenges that come with deploying AI in such critical sectors.

CHAPTER 8: AI IN FINANCE: TRADING, FRAUD DETECTION, AND BEYOND

Artificial Intelligence (AI) is playing an increasingly vital role in the financial sector, transforming how companies manage risks, detect fraud, and optimize investments. Financial institutions are leveraging AI to automate trading strategies, improve credit scoring, and detect suspicious activities with unprecedented speed and accuracy. In this chapter, we'll explore how AI is being applied in the finance industry, covering stock trading, fraud detection, and credit scoring, and take a closer look at real-world applications like **robo-advisors** and **personal finance management apps** that are changing the way individuals manage their money.

The Role of AI in the Financial Sector

Finance has always been driven by data. Stock prices, market trends, credit scores, transaction histories—all of these form the foundation of financial decision-making. However, the volume of data generated by global financial markets is staggering, and it's far beyond what human analysts can process efficiently. AI is perfectly suited to the financial industry because of its ability to analyze massive amounts of data quickly and accurately, identify patterns, and make predictions.

How AI Enhances Decision-Making in Finance

AI systems in finance use **machine learning** and **predictive analytics** to help financial institutions make faster and more informed decisions. These systems can:

- **Identify trends and patterns** in historical data to make predictions about future market movements.
- **Detect anomalies** that could indicate fraudulent activities.
- **Automate routine tasks** like portfolio rebalancing, risk management, and client communication.

By automating and enhancing these processes, AI can not only improve operational efficiency but also uncover new insights that were previously too complex or time-consuming for human analysts to detect.

The Competitive Edge of AI in Finance

The ability to process data faster than humans and with fewer errors gives financial firms that adopt AI a competitive edge. Whether it's making split-second trading decisions or flagging potential fraud before it occurs, AI-driven systems have become indispensable tools in the financial sector. Furthermore, AI can help democratize financial services by providing tailored advice and automation for individual users, whether through robo-advisors or personal finance apps.

How AI is Used in Stock Trading, Credit Scoring, and Fraud Detection

Now, let's take a closer look at three key areas where AI is making a significant impact in the financial sector: **stock trading**, **credit scoring**, and **fraud detection**.

1. AI in Stock Trading

In the fast-paced world of stock trading, AI is revolutionizing how traders buy and sell assets. **Algorithmic trading** (also known as **automated trading** or **high-frequency trading**) uses AI algorithms to analyze market data and execute trades at lightning speed. These algorithms are designed to identify patterns, react to market fluctuations, and execute trades without human intervention.

How AI Powers Algorithmic Trading

AI in stock trading works by:

1. **Analyzing historical market data**: AI algorithms use machine learning to study vast amounts of historical data, such as stock prices, market trends, and economic indicators. This helps the system recognize patterns that precede certain market movements.

2. **Predicting price movements**: Once trained on historical data, AI systems can make predictions about how stock prices will change based on current market

conditions. For instance, if the AI detects that certain market factors often lead to a rise in tech stocks, it can predict similar movements in the future.

3. **Executing trades automatically**: Algorithmic trading platforms use these predictions to buy or sell assets within milliseconds of detecting a profitable opportunity. This speed is crucial, especially in high-frequency trading, where large volumes of trades are executed in a fraction of a second.

The Advantages of AI in Trading

- **Speed**: AI can execute trades much faster than human traders, enabling financial firms to capitalize on market opportunities before prices change.

- **Emotionless decision-making**: Unlike human traders, AI doesn't make emotional decisions. It strictly follows data and patterns, reducing the risk of irrational behavior during market volatility.

- **24/7 operation**: AI algorithms can operate around the clock, analyzing global markets and executing trades even when human traders are asleep.

However, while AI-driven trading systems have transformed the financial markets, they also pose risks, such as amplifying volatility during market crashes. For instance, during the **Flash Crash of 2010**, algorithmic trading systems contributed to a sudden drop in the U.S. stock market. As a result, regulators and financial institutions are increasingly focused on ensuring that AI-driven trading systems are designed responsibly.

2. AI in Credit Scoring

Traditionally, credit scores were determined by human analysts who assessed a borrower's financial history, income, and debt levels to determine creditworthiness. AI is now automating this process, offering more accurate and faster credit scoring models that can analyze far more data points than traditional methods.

How AI Enhances Credit Scoring

AI-based credit scoring systems evaluate a wide range of factors, including:

- **Financial data**: Traditional data points like payment history, outstanding loans, and income.
- **Alternative data**: AI can also assess alternative data, such as social media behavior, e-commerce activity, and even smartphone usage patterns, to generate a more comprehensive picture of a borrower's financial responsibility.

By analyzing both traditional and alternative data, AI systems can generate more accurate credit scores, particularly for individuals who may not have extensive financial histories (e.g., younger consumers or those without significant credit card usage). AI models can also continuously update credit scores in real time as new data becomes available.

Real-World Impact: AI-Based Credit Scoring

Zest AI is one example of a company using AI to improve credit scoring. By analyzing thousands of data points, Zest AI's platform provides more inclusive and accurate credit scores, helping lenders make better-informed decisions and giving more people access to loans. Their system has been shown to reduce loan defaults while increasing loan approval rates.

AI-driven credit scoring is also being used to reduce bias in lending. Traditional credit scoring models have been criticized for perpetuating biases, particularly against minority and low-income borrowers. AI models, by analyzing a wider range of data points, have the potential to be more equitable—although the challenge remains to ensure that the models themselves do not introduce new forms of bias.

3. AI in Fraud Detection

Fraud is a major concern in the financial industry, with billions of dollars lost annually to various forms of fraud, from credit card fraud to identity theft. AI is now at the forefront of detecting and preventing fraud by analyzing transactions and user behavior in real time.

How AI Detects Fraud

AI-powered fraud detection systems use **machine learning** to analyze vast amounts of transaction data and flag unusual or suspicious behavior. These systems continuously learn from historical fraud patterns to improve their accuracy and reduce false positives (legitimate transactions incorrectly flagged as fraudulent). Here's how AI enhances fraud detection:

1. **Transaction monitoring**: AI algorithms can monitor millions of transactions in real time, identifying patterns that may indicate fraud. For example, if a user in New York suddenly makes a large purchase in a different country, AI may flag the transaction as suspicious.

2. **Behavioral analysis**: In addition to transaction data, AI can analyze user behavior, such as login patterns, IP addresses, and device usage. If a user's behavior deviates from their normal habits—such as logging in from an unfamiliar location—the system can flag the account for further review.

3. **Continuous learning**: Fraudsters are constantly evolving their tactics, but AI systems can learn from new data and adapt to emerging fraud techniques, improving their detection capabilities over time.

PayPal, one of the world's largest online payment platforms, uses AI to detect fraud and protect its users. By analyzing thousands of data points for each transaction—such as the user's purchase history, location, and device—PayPal's AI system can flag potentially fraudulent transactions in real time. This has enabled PayPal to reduce fraud losses while maintaining a high level of user trust.

Real-World Example: Robo-Advisors and Personal Finance Management Apps

AI isn't just transforming institutional finance; it's also changing how individuals manage their personal finances. Two key innovations in this space are **robo-advisors** and **personal finance management apps**, both of which use AI to provide financial advice, manage investments, and help users achieve their financial goals.

Robo-Advisors: Automating Investment Management

Robo-advisors are AI-powered platforms that provide automated investment management services. They use algorithms to create and manage a personalized investment portfolio based on the user's financial goals, risk tolerance, and time horizon. Robo-advisors are typically more affordable than traditional human financial advisors and are accessible to a wider range of investors.

How Robo-Advisors Work

1. **User profiling**: The robo-advisor begins by collecting information about the user's financial goals, risk tolerance, and investment preferences through a questionnaire.

2. **Portfolio creation**: Based on this information, the robo-advisor's algorithm creates a diversified investment portfolio, typically consisting of a mix of stocks, bonds, and other assets.

3. **Automated rebalancing**: Once the portfolio is set up, the robo-advisor continuously monitors market conditions and automatically rebalances the portfolio to maintain the target asset allocation. This ensures that the user's portfolio stays aligned with their financial goals.

4. **Low fees**: One of the biggest advantages of robo-advisors is that they typically charge lower fees than traditional advisors, making them more accessible to everyday investors.

Real-World Example: Betterment

Betterment is one of the most popular robo-advisors in the world. Using AI algorithms, Betterment builds and manages investment portfolios for users, offering features like automatic portfolio rebalancing and tax-loss harvesting. The platform is designed to optimize returns while keeping costs low, making it an attractive option for investors who want a hands-off approach to managing their money.

Personal Finance Management Apps: AI for Budgeting and Saving

Personal finance management apps like **Mint, YNAB** (You Need A Budget), and **Emma** use AI to help users manage their finances by tracking spending, creating budgets, and offering personalized financial advice. These apps connect to users' bank accounts and credit cards, automatically categorizing transactions and providing insights into spending habits.

How AI Powers Personal Finance Apps

1. **Transaction categorization**: AI algorithms categorize transactions into spending categories (e.g., groceries, entertainment, utilities) to give users a clear picture of where their money is going.

2. **Budgeting and goal-setting**: Based on the user's spending patterns, AI-powered apps can suggest budgets and help users set financial goals, such as saving for a vacation or paying off debt.

3. **Spending alerts and insights**: AI can also identify unusual spending patterns and send alerts if the user is overspending or approaching their budget limits.

Some apps even offer tips for reducing expenses or increasing savings.

Real-World Example: Mint

Mint is one of the most widely used personal finance apps. It uses AI to track spending, categorize transactions, and provide users with a personalized overview of their finances. By analyzing spending habits, Mint can suggest ways to save money, warn users when they're overspending, and help them create budgets that align with their financial goals.

Conclusion

AI is reshaping the financial sector in profound ways. From improving the speed and accuracy of stock trading to enhancing fraud detection and automating investment management, AI is helping both institutions and individuals make better financial decisions. Through real-world applications like **robo-advisors** and **personal finance management apps**, AI is also democratizing financial services, making them more accessible and affordable for everyday users.

As AI continues to evolve, we can expect even more advanced financial tools that offer personalized, data-driven advice and help users optimize their financial lives. The future of finance is increasingly automated, intelligent, and efficient, thanks to the power of AI.

CHAPTER 9: AI IN AUTONOMOUS VEHICLES: THE FUTURE OF TRANSPORTATION

The rise of **autonomous vehicles (AVs)** is one of the most exciting and transformative applications of artificial intelligence (AI). Self-driving cars promise to reshape the way we think about transportation, potentially reducing traffic accidents, increasing road safety, and providing new mobility solutions for people around the world. In this chapter, we'll explore the technology behind self-driving cars, focusing on how AI processes data from various sensors and makes decisions in real time. We'll also examine real-world examples like **Tesla's Autopilot** and **Google's Waymo**, two of the most advanced autonomous vehicle projects in development today.

Overview of Self-Driving Car Technology

At the core of self-driving car technology is **AI**, which allows vehicles to navigate and operate without human intervention. Autonomous vehicles are equipped with a range of sensors and advanced algorithms that work together to perceive their surroundings, make driving decisions, and execute maneuvers safely. The goal of these systems is to replicate, and eventually surpass, human driving capabilities.

Levels of Autonomy

The **Society of Automotive Engineers (SAE)** defines six levels of driving automation, from Level 0 (no automation) to Level 5 (full automation). Here's a quick overview of these levels:

- **Level 0**: No Automation – The driver is fully responsible for driving tasks.
- **Level 1**: Driver Assistance – The car can assist with basic tasks like steering or acceleration, but the driver is still responsible.
- **Level 2**: Partial Automation – The car can control steering, acceleration, and braking, but the driver must monitor the environment and be ready to take over.
- **Level 3**: Conditional Automation – The car can handle most driving tasks in specific conditions, but the driver must take over when required.
- **Level 4**: High Automation – The car can drive itself without human intervention in certain environments (e.g., highways or cities).
- **Level 5**: Full Automation – The car is fully autonomous and capable of driving in all conditions without any human input.

While Level 5 vehicles are the ultimate goal, most current self-driving systems, including **Tesla's Autopilot** and **Google Waymo**, operate at Levels 2 and 4, respectively, with Level 5 still in the research and development phase.

Key Components of Self-Driving Cars

Self-driving cars rely on a combination of sensors, machine learning algorithms, and real-time decision-making systems to operate safely and efficiently. The key components that make this possible include:

1. **Sensors**: Self-driving cars are equipped with a variety of sensors that help them perceive their surroundings. These include:

   o **Cameras**: Used to capture visual information about the environment, such as road signs, lane markings, traffic lights, and other vehicles.

   o **Radar**: Measures the distance and speed of surrounding objects, such as other cars, pedestrians, and obstacles.

   o **Lidar (Light Detection and Ranging)**: Uses lasers to create a 3D map of the vehicle's surroundings, helping the car detect objects in all directions.

- o **Ultrasonic sensors**: Typically used for close-range detection, such as parking assistance and detecting nearby objects at low speeds.

2. **AI and Machine Learning Algorithms**: The AI in autonomous vehicles is responsible for processing the data collected by sensors, recognizing patterns, and making decisions. Machine learning models help the vehicle "learn" from real-world driving experiences, improving its ability to navigate complex scenarios over time.

3. **Control Systems**: Once the AI has processed the data and made a decision, the vehicle's control systems execute those actions. These systems control the car's steering, acceleration, and braking, allowing the vehicle to follow the AI's commands.

How AI Processes Data from Sensors and Makes Decisions

The ability of self-driving cars to operate autonomously is made possible by AI systems that process the vast amounts of data generated by sensors. These AI systems must perform three critical tasks: **perception**, **decision-making**, and **action**. Let's break down how AI processes sensor data to navigate the world.

1. Perception: Understanding the Environment

The first task for AI in an autonomous vehicle is **perception**— understanding what's happening around the car. This involves processing data from the vehicle's sensors to detect and classify objects, recognize road conditions, and identify potential hazards. The car's sensors continuously feed raw data to the AI, which must then interpret it in real time.

- **Cameras** capture images of the road, traffic signals, pedestrians, and other vehicles. The AI system uses **computer vision** algorithms to process these images, identifying objects and interpreting road signs or traffic lights.

- **Lidar** and **radar** provide information about the distance, speed, and position of objects. Lidar creates detailed 3D maps of the environment, while radar is used to track moving objects like cars and pedestrians.

- **Sensor fusion**: AI systems combine data from multiple sensors to create a comprehensive view of the environment. For example, data from cameras might be fused with Lidar data to ensure accurate object detection even in poor lighting conditions or during bad weather.

Example of Perception in Action:

When a self-driving car approaches an intersection, its cameras detect the traffic light, its Lidar scans the surrounding area for other vehicles, and its radar tracks the speed of nearby cars. The AI system then interprets this data to understand whether it's safe to proceed or if the vehicle should stop.

2. Decision-Making: Choosing the Best Course of Action

Once the AI system has a clear understanding of its surroundings, it must decide what to do next. This is where **decision-making algorithms** come into play. The AI system uses machine learning models and predefined rules to evaluate different actions and choose the safest and most efficient option.

- **Path planning**: The AI system determines the best route for the vehicle to follow, considering factors such as the destination, road conditions, and traffic. This involves calculating the optimal trajectory for the vehicle while avoiding obstacles.

- **Predictive modeling**: AI systems use predictive models to anticipate the behavior of other road users. For example, if the car detects a pedestrian near a crosswalk, it can predict whether the person is likely to step into the road, allowing the car to slow down or stop in time.

- **Prioritization**: The AI system must prioritize different tasks, such as stopping at a red light, avoiding a cyclist, or merging onto a highway. Machine learning algorithms help the car weigh these decisions and select the appropriate action based on the situation.

Example of Decision-Making in Action:

If a self-driving car is driving in heavy traffic and detects a slow-moving vehicle ahead, it must decide whether to slow down or change lanes to maintain speed. The AI system analyzes the traffic patterns, checks if the adjacent lane is clear, and calculates whether a lane change is the safest and most efficient maneuver.

3. Action: Controlling the Vehicle

Once the AI system has made a decision, the vehicle's **control systems** take over to execute the required actions. These systems control the car's steering, acceleration, and braking to follow the AI's instructions.

- **Steering**: If the AI decides to change lanes, the control system adjusts the steering to guide the vehicle into the new lane smoothly.
- **Acceleration and braking**: The AI system controls the car's speed by adjusting the acceleration or braking. For example, if the AI detects that the car is approaching a stop sign, it instructs the braking system to slow the vehicle down and stop it safely.

These control systems must operate with extreme precision, as even a small error in braking or steering could result in an accident.

Real-World Example: Tesla and Google Waymo Autonomous Vehicles

Two of the most prominent players in the autonomous vehicle industry are **Tesla** and **Waymo** (a subsidiary of Alphabet, Google's parent company). Both companies have made significant strides in self-driving technology, but they take different approaches to autonomy. Let's examine how Tesla and Waymo use AI to power their self-driving cars and the progress they've made in the real world.

Tesla: Autopilot and Full-Self Driving (FSD)

Tesla, led by CEO Elon Musk, has been a pioneer in bringing semi-autonomous driving features to the consumer market. Tesla's **Autopilot** and **Full-Self Driving (FSD)** systems use AI and a suite of cameras, radar, and ultrasonic sensors to assist with driving tasks.

How Tesla's AI System Works:

- **Cameras and sensors**: Tesla vehicles rely heavily on cameras to capture visual information about the road. The company uses a **vision-based approach**, meaning it focuses on using camera data, supplemented by radar and ultrasonic sensors, to perceive the environment.
- **Neural networks**: Tesla's AI system is built on deep learning **neural networks** that process the visual data from the cameras and make decisions based on the patterns the system has learned. Tesla's neural networks are trained on massive datasets collected from its fleet of vehicles, which provide real-world driving data in various conditions.
- **Driver assistance**: Tesla's Autopilot offers features such as **adaptive cruise control**, **lane-keeping**, and **automatic lane**

changes. While Tesla vehicles are capable of handling many driving tasks autonomously, drivers are still required to keep their hands on the wheel and be ready to take over at any moment.

- **Full-Self Driving (FSD) Beta**: Tesla is gradually rolling out its **FSD Beta** software, which is designed to handle complex urban driving scenarios such as navigating through traffic, making turns at intersections, and parking. However, Tesla's FSD is not yet at Level 5 autonomy, meaning human oversight is still required.

Real-World Example:

Tesla's Autopilot system has been used by millions of drivers, and the company claims that its AI-powered safety features (like **automatic emergency braking**) have reduced the likelihood of accidents. However, Tesla has faced scrutiny and controversy, particularly around how it markets its FSD feature, as some drivers mistakenly assume the system is fully autonomous when it still requires human supervision.

Waymo: Full Self-Driving Taxis

Waymo, formerly known as Google's self-driving car project, is at the forefront of fully autonomous driving technology. Unlike Tesla's vision-based approach, Waymo uses a combination of **Lidar, radar, and cameras** to create a detailed 3D map of its surroundings. Waymo's focus is on achieving Level 4 and Level 5 autonomy, where vehicles can drive themselves without any human intervention.

How Waymo's AI System Works:

- **Lidar**: Waymo relies heavily on Lidar technology to create a detailed 3D map of the environment. This allows the vehicle to detect and track objects at long distances, even in low-light or adverse weather conditions.
- **Machine learning**: Waymo's AI system uses **deep learning** to analyze sensor data and predict the behavior of other road users. The system has been trained on millions of miles of driving data collected in real-world conditions, enabling it to handle a wide range of driving scenarios.
- **Fleet learning**: Similar to Tesla, Waymo's vehicles continuously collect data to improve the AI's performance. This data is shared across Waymo's fleet, allowing the entire system to learn from the experiences of individual vehicles.

Real-World Example: Waymo One

Waymo launched **Waymo One**, the world's first fully autonomous taxi service, in **Chandler, Arizona**. The service operates without a human driver and allows passengers to hail a ride via a mobile app. Waymo's self-driving cars are equipped with redundant safety systems and have successfully completed thousands of rides without human intervention.

Waymo's approach represents the closest example of a Level 4 autonomous system currently in operation, although it is limited to specific geographic areas where the system has been extensively tested.

Conclusion

AI is driving the future of transportation, and autonomous vehicles are at the forefront of this transformation. By processing data from cameras, Lidar, radar, and other sensors, AI systems enable self-driving cars to perceive their environment, make real-time decisions, and safely navigate complex road conditions. Companies like **Tesla** and **Waymo** are leading the charge, each taking a unique approach to developing autonomous driving technology.

While Tesla is focused on gradually improving driver-assistance features through its Autopilot and Full-Self Driving systems, Waymo is working toward full autonomy with its self-driving taxis. Both companies are making significant strides, but full Level 5 autonomy, where cars can drive themselves in all conditions without any human input, remains an ambitious goal that will require further advancements in AI, safety, and regulation.

In the next chapter, we will explore how AI is being used in entertainment, from content recommendation algorithms on platforms like Netflix to AI-generated art and music.

CHAPTER 10: MACHINE LEARNING IN BUSINESS: OPTIMIZING OPERATIONS AND CUSTOMER EXPERIENCE

Machine learning (ML) and artificial intelligence (AI) are transforming the way businesses operate, helping companies optimize everything from supply chains to customer support. AI's ability to process vast amounts of data, identify patterns, and make predictions allows businesses to improve efficiency, reduce costs, and enhance customer experiences. In this chapter, we will explore how businesses are using AI to streamline operations, improve customer engagement, and drive innovation. We'll also take a closer look at specific applications of AI in **logistics and supply chain optimization** and **customer support through chatbots and virtual agents**.

How Businesses Use AI to Improve Efficiency and Customer Engagement

In the age of digital transformation, companies are increasingly turning to AI and machine learning to stay competitive and deliver better services. By leveraging AI, businesses can automate routine tasks, gain deeper insights from data, and make smarter decisions.

Here are some of the key ways AI is being used to improve efficiency and customer engagement across industries:

1. Automating Repetitive Tasks

One of the most common uses of AI in business is automating repetitive, time-consuming tasks. Machine learning algorithms can handle tasks like data entry, inventory management, and even financial analysis, allowing human employees to focus on more complex and creative work.

- **Example**: In finance, AI systems can process and reconcile invoices, detect errors in accounting, and manage payroll automatically, reducing the need for manual intervention.

2. Predictive Analytics for Smarter Decision-Making

AI-powered predictive analytics tools help businesses anticipate future trends, customer behaviors, and potential operational bottlenecks. These insights allow companies to make data-driven decisions, optimize resource allocation, and identify new growth opportunities.

- **Example**: Retailers use predictive analytics to forecast demand for products, ensuring they stock the right items at the right time. This not only minimizes waste but also improves customer satisfaction by reducing stockouts.

3. Enhancing Customer Engagement

AI-driven solutions like personalized recommendations, dynamic pricing, and targeted marketing campaigns help businesses engage customers more effectively. Machine learning algorithms analyze customer behavior, preferences, and purchasing history to deliver tailored experiences that keep customers coming back.

- **Example**: E-commerce platforms like **Amazon** use AI to recommend products based on previous searches, purchases, and browsing habits. These personalized recommendations account for a significant portion of Amazon's revenue, as they improve customer engagement and drive higher sales.

4. Improving Employee Productivity

AI tools are also being deployed to enhance employee productivity by providing real-time insights and automating administrative tasks. For example, AI-powered virtual assistants can help manage schedules, answer routine questions, and streamline communication, freeing up employees to focus on higher-value tasks.

- **Example**: At **Microsoft**, AI-based tools like **Cortana** assist employees with managing their emails, scheduling meetings, and organizing tasks, reducing time spent on administrative duties.

5. Optimizing Resource Management

AI systems can optimize the use of resources—whether that's employee time, physical inventory, or energy consumption. This is particularly beneficial in industries with complex operations like manufacturing, logistics, and retail, where optimizing processes can significantly impact profitability.

- **Example**: In the energy sector, AI systems can predict energy demand and adjust supply dynamically, reducing waste and improving efficiency in power grids.

As we'll explore in the next sections, AI's ability to optimize operations extends beyond improving business processes. It's also revolutionizing logistics and supply chain management—two critical areas for many industries.

AI in Logistics and Supply Chain Optimization

The global supply chain is a complex network of suppliers, manufacturers, warehouses, and distributors that work together to deliver goods and services to consumers. Managing this network efficiently requires careful coordination and the ability to predict demand, track inventory, and respond to changes in real time. AI and machine learning are becoming essential tools for optimizing logistics and supply chain management, helping companies reduce costs, minimize delays, and improve operational resilience.

How AI is Transforming Logistics and Supply Chains

1. **Demand Forecasting and Inventory Management** One of the most important uses of AI in logistics is **demand forecasting**—predicting how much of a product will be

needed at a specific time and place. By analyzing historical sales data, seasonality, market trends, and even external factors like weather, machine learning models can forecast demand with greater accuracy than traditional methods.

- **Impact on Inventory Management**: With more accurate demand forecasts, businesses can maintain optimal inventory levels, reducing the risk of overstocking or stockouts. This leads to more efficient use of warehouse space, lower storage costs, and improved customer satisfaction.

Real-World Example: Walmart

Walmart, one of the largest retailers in the world, uses AI to forecast demand and optimize its supply chain. By analyzing massive datasets, including point-of-sale data, weather patterns, and market trends, Walmart can predict demand for specific products in different regions. This allows the company to adjust inventory levels in real time, ensuring products are available when and where they're needed, while minimizing excess inventory.

2. **Route Optimization and Transportation Management**
   AI plays a critical role in **route optimization**, helping logistics companies determine the most efficient paths for delivering goods. Machine learning

algorithms analyze traffic patterns, road conditions, fuel consumption, and delivery schedules to minimize travel time and reduce costs.

- **Dynamic routing**: AI can also adjust routes in real time based on changing conditions, such as accidents, weather delays, or road closures. This flexibility ensures that deliveries remain on schedule and that transportation resources are used efficiently.

Real-World Example: UPS

UPS uses an AI-powered system called **ORION (On-Road Integrated Optimization and Navigation)** to optimize delivery routes for its drivers. ORION uses machine learning algorithms to analyze factors like traffic, fuel costs, and package delivery deadlines, allowing UPS to create the most efficient route for each driver. Since its implementation, ORION has helped UPS save millions of miles and gallons of fuel each year, reducing operational costs and environmental impact.

3. **Warehouse Automation and Robotics** AI-powered **robots** and **automated systems** are increasingly being used in warehouses to streamline the picking, packing, and sorting processes. These systems use machine learning to analyze real-time data on inventory levels

and order demand, allowing them to work efficiently without human intervention.

- **Automated storage and retrieval systems (ASRS)**: These AI-driven systems are used in large warehouses to store and retrieve products with high precision and speed, reducing the need for manual labor and improving efficiency.

Real-World Example: Amazon

Amazon is a leader in warehouse automation, using AI-powered robots to improve operational efficiency. In Amazon's fulfillment centers, robots are used to move products from storage to packing stations, where they are prepared for shipment. The company's **Kiva robots** use AI to optimize their movements, reducing the time it takes to fulfill orders and minimizing errors. This level of automation enables Amazon to meet high consumer demand while keeping operational costs low.

4. **Supply Chain Risk Management** In today's interconnected global economy, supply chains are vulnerable to disruptions caused by natural disasters, geopolitical events, and other unforeseen circumstances. AI helps companies mitigate these risks by monitoring real-time data and providing early warnings of potential disruptions.

- **AI-driven supply chain visibility**: Machine learning algorithms can analyze data from suppliers, manufacturers, and logistics providers to detect anomalies or disruptions in the supply chain. This allows businesses to respond quickly and implement contingency plans, such as rerouting shipments or sourcing alternative suppliers.

Real-World Example: IBM Watson in Supply Chain Risk Management

IBM Watson offers an AI-powered supply chain risk management platform that helps businesses anticipate and respond to disruptions. By analyzing vast amounts of data from external sources, including news reports, weather patterns, and political events, Watson can predict potential risks and recommend actions to mitigate them. Companies using this system can reduce the impact of supply chain disruptions, ensuring that goods are delivered on time even in challenging circumstances.

Real-World Example: AI in Customer Support via Chatbots and Virtual Agents

Customer support is a critical part of any business, and AI is revolutionizing how companies interact with their customers. **Chatbots** and **virtual agents** powered by AI are becoming increasingly popular tools for handling customer inquiries, providing 24/7 support, and improving overall customer experience. These AI-driven systems offer real-time assistance, reducing wait times and improving customer satisfaction.

How AI-Powered Chatbots and Virtual Agents Work

AI chatbots and virtual agents use **natural language processing (NLP)** and **machine learning** to understand and respond to customer inquiries in a human-like manner. Here's how they work:

1. **Understanding Customer Queries**: Chatbots use NLP to interpret text or spoken language, allowing them to understand what the customer is asking for. For example, if a customer types, "I need help with my order," the chatbot can identify the intent behind the message and take appropriate action.

2. **Providing Automated Responses**: Based on the intent of the query, the chatbot searches its database for the most relevant response. This could involve providing information about a product, troubleshooting an issue, or guiding the customer through a process.

3. **Escalating Complex Issues**: If the chatbot cannot resolve the issue or if the customer's inquiry is too complex, the system can escalate the query to a human agent. This ensures that customers receive the appropriate level of support while minimizing the workload for customer service teams.

Benefits of AI in Customer Support

1. **24/7 Availability**: AI chatbots are available around the clock, allowing customers to get help whenever they need it, without waiting for business hours.
2. **Faster Response Times**: By automating routine inquiries, chatbots can respond to customers instantly, reducing wait times and improving the overall customer experience.
3. **Cost Efficiency**: Chatbots can handle large volumes of customer inquiries simultaneously, reducing the need for large customer support teams and lowering operational costs.

Real-World Example: Chatbots in Action – H&M

The global fashion retailer **H&M** uses an AI-powered chatbot to assist customers with their shopping experience. The chatbot can answer questions about product availability, help customers find items that match their preferences, and provide personalized recommendations based on previous purchases or browsing history. By offering instant responses to customer inquiries, H&M's chatbot improves customer satisfaction while reducing the workload for human agents.

Another example is **LivePerson**, a company that provides AI-powered customer engagement solutions. LivePerson's chatbots are designed to handle complex customer service issues, such as troubleshooting technical problems or processing returns, and can escalate more challenging cases to human agents when necessary.

Virtual Agents in Financial Services: Bank of America's Erica

In the financial sector, **Bank of America** has developed an AI-driven virtual assistant named **Erica**. Erica helps customers manage their accounts, make payments, track spending, and even provide personalized financial advice. Using machine learning and NLP, Erica can understand and respond to customer inquiries via voice, text, or the bank's mobile app. Since its launch, Erica has been widely adopted by Bank of America's customers, helping the bank deliver more personalized, efficient customer service.

Conclusion

AI and machine learning are playing a transformative role in business, helping companies optimize their operations and deliver better customer experiences. From logistics and supply chain management to customer support, AI is driving efficiency and improving decision-making across industries. In logistics, machine learning algorithms help companies forecast demand, optimize routes, and manage inventory, while chatbots and virtual agents provide fast, 24/7 support to customers, reducing costs and improving satisfaction.

As AI continues to evolve, businesses will increasingly rely on these technologies to stay competitive and meet the ever-growing demands of customers. The future of business lies in leveraging AI not only to streamline operations but also to build stronger, more personalized relationships with customers.

CHAPTER 11: DEEP LEARNING DEMYSTIFIED

Artificial intelligence (AI) has made tremendous progress in recent years, thanks in large part to **deep learning**. Deep learning, a subset of machine learning, is powering some of the most impressive advancements in AI, from facial recognition to image processing. In this chapter, we will demystify deep learning by explaining its fundamental principles and how it differs from traditional machine learning. We will also examine a real-world example of deep learning in action—**facial recognition** and **image processing**, such as the technology used by Facebook and other platforms.

Introduction to Deep Learning and Neural Networks

Deep learning is a specialized area of machine learning that focuses on using artificial **neural networks** to model complex patterns in data. These neural networks are designed to mimic the structure and functioning of the human brain, allowing machines to process and learn from large amounts of data. Deep learning has been particularly effective in tasks involving image and speech recognition, natural language processing, and even autonomous vehicles.

Neural Networks: The Foundation of Deep Learning

At the heart of deep learning are **neural networks**—computational models inspired by the structure of biological brains. These networks consist of layers of interconnected nodes (also called **neurons**) that process input data, transform it, and produce an output. Here's a simplified breakdown of how neural networks work:

1. **Input layer**: This is where the raw data enters the network. For example, if you're training a neural network to recognize images of cats and dogs, the input layer would receive the pixel values of an image.

2. **Hidden layers**: Between the input and output layers are one or more hidden layers, where the network performs complex mathematical operations. Each neuron in a hidden layer receives inputs, processes them, and passes the result to the next layer. These hidden layers allow the network to learn representations of the data—such as the shapes, edges, or textures in an image.

3. **Output layer**: The final layer produces the network's output. In an image classification task, the output layer would indicate the probability of the input image belonging to a particular class (e.g., cat or dog).

The key to the power of neural networks is their ability to **learn** from data. Initially, the network's predictions may be inaccurate, but through a process called **backpropagation**, the network adjusts its internal parameters (called **weights**) to improve its accuracy over time. The more data the network processes, the better it becomes at making correct predictions.

How Deep Learning Differs from Traditional Machine Learning

To understand the significance of deep learning, it's essential to know how it differs from **traditional machine learning**.

1. Feature Extraction

One of the primary differences between traditional machine learning and deep learning is how they handle **feature extraction**—the process of identifying and selecting the most relevant characteristics of the data to make accurate predictions.

- **Traditional machine learning**: In traditional machine learning, feature extraction is often done manually by data scientists or engineers. For example, when building a machine learning model to classify images, experts might have to define features like color, texture, and shape to help the model distinguish between different objects. This manual process can be time-consuming and requires domain expertise.

- **Deep learning**: In deep learning, feature extraction is done automatically by the neural network. The network learns to identify the important features of the data during training, without requiring human intervention. For example, a deep learning model trained on images of cats and dogs will automatically learn to recognize features like fur patterns, ear shapes, and body outlines, improving its classification accuracy. This ability to learn from raw data without manual feature engineering is one of the major advantages of deep learning.

2. Complexity of Models

Traditional machine learning algorithms, such as **decision trees** or **support vector machines (SVMs)**, are relatively simple compared to deep learning models. While these algorithms are effective for many tasks, they can struggle with complex data like images, video, or audio.

- **Traditional machine learning**: In traditional machine learning, models are often shallow, meaning they have only a few layers of decision-making. This limits their ability to capture intricate patterns in data.
- **Deep learning**: Deep learning models, on the other hand, are designed with multiple hidden layers (hence the term "deep"). Each layer extracts increasingly complex features from the data, allowing the model to recognize higher-level patterns. For example, in image recognition, the first few layers might detect basic edges, while deeper layers detect

more complex shapes and objects. This multi-layered structure makes deep learning highly effective for tasks like image classification and natural language processing.

3. Data Requirements

While deep learning has proven to be extremely powerful, it also comes with higher data requirements.

- **Traditional machine learning**: Traditional machine learning algorithms often work well with smaller datasets, provided that the data is well-structured and feature selection is done properly.

- **Deep learning**: Deep learning models, particularly neural networks, perform best with **large datasets**. Because these models have so many layers and parameters to train, they require vast amounts of data to avoid overfitting (when a model performs well on training data but poorly on unseen data). This is why deep learning has become more feasible in recent years, thanks to the availability of big data and advances in computational power.

4. Computational Power

- **Traditional machine learning**: Most traditional machine learning algorithms can be run on standard computers without requiring extensive computational resources. They can be trained relatively quickly, even on smaller machines.

- **Deep learning**: Deep learning models, especially deep neural networks, require significant computational power. Training these models often involves using specialized hardware like **Graphics Processing Units (GPUs)** or **Tensor Processing Units (TPUs)**, which are designed to handle the massive number of calculations involved in training deep neural networks. As a result, deep learning can be more resource-intensive, but it offers much higher accuracy and scalability in tasks like image processing, speech recognition, and language translation.

Real-World Example: AI in Facial Recognition and Image Processing (e.g., Facebook)

One of the most well-known applications of deep learning is **facial recognition**, a technology that allows computers to identify and verify individuals based on their facial features. Facial recognition is widely used across industries, from security and law enforcement to social media platforms like **Facebook**, where it helps users tag friends in photos. Let's take a closer look at how deep learning powers facial recognition and image processing.

How Facial Recognition Works

Facial recognition technology uses deep learning models to analyze and compare facial features in images or video. The process typically involves the following steps:

1. **Face Detection**: The first step is detecting the presence of a face in an image or video feed. Deep learning models, often using **convolutional neural networks (CNNs)**, scan the image and locate the region containing a face.

2. **Feature Extraction**: Once the face is detected, the neural network extracts key features of the face, such as the distance between the eyes, the shape of the jawline, or the contours of the nose. These features are then transformed into a mathematical representation, known as a **facial embedding**, which uniquely identifies the individual.

3. **Comparison and Matching**: To recognize a person, the system compares the extracted facial embedding to a database of known faces. If a match is found, the system can identify or verify the individual.

Example: Facebook's Face Recognition Technology

Facebook is a leading example of a platform that uses deep learning for facial recognition. When users upload photos to Facebook, the platform's facial recognition system automatically scans the image to detect and identify the people in it, making tagging easier and faster.

- **How It Works**: Facebook's deep learning model has been trained on millions of images, enabling it to recognize faces with high accuracy. When you upload a photo, the system uses deep learning algorithms to analyze facial features and compare them to the profiles of people in your friend list. If the system identifies a match, it suggests tagging that person.

- **Privacy Considerations**: While Facebook's facial recognition technology has improved user experience by streamlining the photo-tagging process, it has also raised privacy concerns. Critics argue that the widespread use of facial recognition poses risks to individual privacy and security, leading to regulatory scrutiny and, in some cases, legal challenges.

Beyond Facebook: Other Uses of Facial Recognition

Facial recognition technology is also used in a variety of other applications:

- **Security and surveillance**: Airports and government agencies use facial recognition to enhance security, verifying the identity of travelers or identifying individuals on watchlists.

- **Smartphones**: Many smartphones, such as Apple's iPhones, use facial recognition for secure authentication through features like **Face ID**. Face ID uses deep learning to map a user's face in 3D and unlock the phone based on that data.

- **Retail and customer experience**: Some retailers are experimenting with facial recognition to identify repeat customers and provide personalized service based on their preferences and purchase history.

Image Processing: A Broader Application of Deep Learning

In addition to facial recognition, deep learning is widely used for **image processing**—a field that involves analyzing and manipulating images to extract useful information. Deep learning models, particularly **convolutional neural networks (CNNs)**, have revolutionized image processing tasks, including object detection, image classification, and even artistic style transfer.

How CNNs Work in Image Processing

Convolutional neural networks (CNNs) are the go-to deep learning architecture for image-related tasks. Unlike traditional neural networks, CNNs are specifically designed to process grid-like data, such as images, by leveraging the spatial relationships between pixels.

- **Convolution layers**: In a CNN, the **convolution layers** scan the input image, applying filters (or kernels) to detect features like edges, textures, and shapes. These filters move across the image, creating **feature maps** that highlight important patterns in the data.

- **Pooling layers**: **Pooling layers** reduce the dimensionality of the feature maps, helping the model focus on the most important features and reducing computational complexity. This also makes the model more resistant to changes in image orientation or scale.

- **Fully connected layers**: After a series of convolution and pooling layers, the final part of the network, known as the **fully connected layer**, takes the extracted features and makes a prediction. For example, in an image classification task, the output might be a probability distribution indicating the likelihood that the image belongs to a particular class (e.g., cat, dog, or car).

Real-World Applications of Image Processing

- **Medical imaging**: Deep learning is used in medical image analysis to detect diseases like cancer in X-rays, MRIs, and CT scans. AI systems can analyze images much faster than human radiologists and are often able to spot early signs of disease that might be missed by the human eye.

- **Autonomous vehicles**: Self-driving cars use deep learning to process camera feeds and Lidar data, allowing them to detect objects like pedestrians, traffic signs, and other vehicles in real time.

- **AI-generated art**: Deep learning algorithms like **Generative Adversarial Networks (GANs)** are used to create AI-generated art by learning and replicating artistic styles. These systems can even generate entirely new works of art that blend multiple styles or genres.

Conclusion

Deep learning is at the cutting edge of AI, enabling machines to process and learn from complex data in ways that were once thought impossible. By leveraging neural networks, deep learning systems have revolutionized fields like facial recognition, image processing, and autonomous driving. With real-world applications ranging from Facebook's facial recognition technology to medical image analysis and AI-generated art, deep learning is rapidly changing the way we interact with technology.

As data continues to grow in volume and complexity, deep learning will play an increasingly important role in unlocking new possibilities for AI. Whether it's improving the accuracy of medical diagnoses, creating personalized user experiences, or enabling self-driving cars, deep learning is poised to drive the next wave of AI innovation.

CHAPTER 12: ETHICS AND AI: THE MORAL DILEMMAS OF ARTIFICIAL INTELLIGENCE

As artificial intelligence (AI) continues to evolve, it presents not only remarkable opportunities but also significant ethical challenges. From biased algorithms that perpetuate discrimination to facial recognition technologies that risk infringing on privacy rights, the moral implications of AI have become a growing concern. In this chapter, we'll examine the ethical dilemmas surrounding AI, discuss real-world examples of AI bias and misuse, and explore the critical role of human oversight in ensuring that AI systems are developed and deployed responsibly.

Ethical Concerns Around AI: Bias, Discrimination, and Transparency

AI systems, especially those powered by machine learning, are designed to process data and make decisions based on patterns they detect. While this can lead to impressive innovations, it also opens the door to ethical challenges. The most prominent concerns include **algorithmic bias**, **discrimination**, and the need for **transparency** in how AI systems operate.

1. Algorithmic Bias and Discrimination

One of the most pressing ethical concerns with AI is **algorithmic bias**—the phenomenon where AI systems make unfair or prejudiced decisions based on biased training data. Since machine learning models are trained on historical data, they can inherit the biases present in that data, leading to discriminatory outcomes.

How Bias Enters AI Systems

AI systems learn from the data they are given. If that data contains historical biases—whether based on race, gender, age, or other factors—those biases can be encoded into the AI model. As a result, the model might make decisions that reflect or even amplify those biases.

- **Historical data bias**: If an AI system is trained on data where certain groups have been underrepresented or treated unfairly, it may reinforce those patterns. For example, an AI hiring algorithm trained on resumes from a male-dominated industry might favor male candidates over equally qualified female candidates.

- **Model design bias**: Bias can also enter through the design of the algorithm itself. Decisions about what data to include, how to weight certain factors, and how to structure the model can all introduce bias, often unintentionally.

- **Feedback loop bias**: Once an AI system is deployed, it continues to learn from new data. If the system's biased decisions influence the data it receives (e.g., by disproportionately rejecting certain candidates), it can create a **feedback loop** that perpetuates and worsens the bias over time.

2. Lack of Transparency ("Black Box" Problem)

Another significant ethical concern with AI is the **lack of transparency** in how decisions are made. Many AI systems, particularly those based on deep learning, operate as "black boxes," meaning their internal decision-making processes are difficult to understand, even for the developers who created them. This lack of transparency raises concerns about accountability and trust.

- **Opacities in decision-making**: When an AI system denies someone a loan, rejects a job application, or makes an important healthcare decision, it's often unclear why that decision was made. This can lead to frustration and mistrust, especially when individuals feel they have been treated unfairly but cannot get an explanation.

- **Challenges with explainability**: One of the core difficulties in AI ethics is developing systems that are both powerful and explainable. As AI models become more complex, their decisions can be influenced by thousands of factors, making it difficult to offer a clear and concise explanation for why a certain decision was made. This creates a tension between accuracy and interpretability.

3. Privacy Concerns

AI systems, particularly those used in surveillance or data analysis, raise significant concerns about **privacy**. The ability of AI to process massive amounts of personal data—whether from social media, smartphones, or video surveillance—puts individuals at risk of having their privacy invaded.

- **Data collection**: Many AI systems require vast amounts of data to function effectively. In some cases, this data includes sensitive information about individuals' behaviors, preferences, or locations. The collection and storage of this data create opportunities for misuse, whether by governments, corporations, or malicious actors.

- **Surveillance**: The rise of AI-driven surveillance technologies, such as facial recognition, has sparked concerns about mass surveillance and the erosion of personal privacy. As these technologies become more widespread, there is a growing risk that they will be used to monitor individuals without their consent or to track their movements and activities in ways that infringe on their rights.

Real-World Examples: AI Bias in Hiring Algorithms, Facial Recognition Misuse

While AI holds incredible potential, real-world applications have demonstrated the risks of biased algorithms and the misuse of AI technologies. Let's examine two specific examples: **AI bias in hiring algorithms** and the **misuse of facial recognition technology**.

AI Bias in Hiring Algorithms

One of the most well-known examples of AI bias occurred in the use of AI-powered **hiring algorithms**. Several companies have turned to AI to help screen job applicants, aiming to streamline the hiring process by automating resume reviews and candidate evaluations. While this can make hiring more efficient, it has also led to unintended consequences in terms of bias and discrimination.

The Amazon Case

In 2018, **Amazon** made headlines when it was revealed that the company's AI-powered hiring tool was biased against women. The algorithm had been trained on resumes submitted to the company over a 10-year period, during which the tech industry had been predominantly male. As a result, the AI system learned to favor male candidates over female candidates, penalizing resumes that included references to women's colleges or women's sports teams.

- **How it happened**: The AI system was trained on historical hiring data that reflected the gender imbalance in the tech industry. Because the majority of successful candidates in the past were male, the algorithm learned to associate male-dominated language and experience with successful hiring outcomes. Over time, it developed a bias that favored male applicants.

- **Outcome**: Amazon ultimately scrapped the AI hiring tool, recognizing that it could not effectively eliminate the bias. This case highlighted the dangers of relying on biased training data and underscored the importance of careful oversight when developing AI systems for sensitive tasks like hiring.

Broader Implications

The Amazon case is not unique. Similar concerns have been raised about AI systems used in other areas of hiring, such as algorithms that screen video interviews. If not carefully designed and monitored, these systems can perpetuate biases related to race, gender, or socioeconomic background, leading to unfair outcomes for certain groups of candidates.

Facial Recognition Misuse

Facial recognition is another area where AI has raised ethical concerns, particularly regarding privacy and misuse by law enforcement and governments. While facial recognition technology can be used for legitimate purposes—such as securing smartphones or identifying criminals—it also has the potential to be abused, leading to violations of civil liberties and the wrongful targeting of individuals.

Case Study: Law Enforcement and Bias

In the United States, several studies have shown that facial recognition algorithms are more likely to misidentify people of color, particularly Black and Asian individuals. This racial bias in facial recognition systems poses serious risks when the technology is used in law enforcement, as it can lead to false arrests and wrongful surveillance.

- **Example**: A 2019 study conducted by the **National Institute of Standards and Technology (NIST)** found that many commercial facial recognition algorithms had significantly higher error rates when identifying people of color compared to white individuals. This disparity raises concerns about the use of facial recognition in policing, where misidentifications can have life-altering consequences for those targeted.

- **Protests and public backlash**: In 2020, following widespread protests against racial injustice, several major tech companies, including IBM, Amazon, and Microsoft, announced they would suspend or restrict the use of their facial recognition technologies by law enforcement until issues related to bias and privacy could be addressed.

Broader Implications

The misuse of facial recognition technology extends beyond law enforcement. In countries like China, facial recognition is widely used for surveillance, tracking individuals' movements in public spaces and monitoring their behavior. Critics argue that this technology can be used to suppress dissent and infringe on individual freedoms, especially when combined with other surveillance tools like social credit systems.

The Role of Human Oversight in AI

Given the ethical concerns surrounding AI, one of the key solutions is the implementation of **human oversight** to ensure that AI systems are developed and used responsibly. While AI can perform many tasks autonomously, human intervention is necessary to address issues like bias, fairness, and accountability.

1. AI Auditing and Transparency

One of the first steps in ensuring ethical AI is developing mechanisms for **AI auditing** and **transparency**. This involves regular evaluations of AI systems to ensure that they are functioning as intended and that their decisions are fair and unbiased.

- **Transparency requirements**: Companies that use AI should be transparent about how their algorithms make decisions. This includes explaining what data is used, how models are trained, and what criteria are applied in decision-making processes.

- **Algorithmic auditing**: Independent audits of AI systems can help detect biases and flaws that may not be apparent to developers. These audits can involve examining the training data, evaluating the model's performance across different demographic groups, and testing the system under various conditions.

2. Human-in-the-Loop Systems

To prevent AI from making harmful or biased decisions, many companies and institutions are adopting **human-in-the-loop (HITL)** systems. These systems ensure that while AI may assist in decision-making, humans remain in control and can intervene when necessary.

- **Manual reviews**: In sensitive areas like hiring, healthcare, or criminal justice, human reviewers should have the final say on important decisions. For example, if an AI system flags certain job applicants for rejection, a human reviewer can assess whether the decision was fair or biased.

- **Accountability**: Human oversight also ensures accountability. When AI makes decisions that impact people's lives, it's essential that there is a clear path for accountability, meaning that someone is responsible for reviewing the AI's decisions and addressing any mistakes or issues that arise.

3. Ethical AI Development Frameworks

Companies and organizations are increasingly adopting **ethical AI frameworks** to guide the responsible development and deployment of AI technologies. These frameworks typically include principles such as fairness, accountability, transparency, and privacy.

- **Examples of ethical AI frameworks**: Companies like Google and Microsoft have published AI ethics guidelines to ensure that their AI systems are developed with a focus on minimizing harm and maximizing fairness. These frameworks emphasize the importance of diversity in AI teams, regular bias testing, and the responsible use of data.
- **Regulatory frameworks**: Governments are also starting to introduce regulations to govern the use of AI, particularly in areas like facial recognition, data privacy, and algorithmic decision-making. These regulations aim to ensure that AI systems are transparent, accountable, and fair, with appropriate safeguards in place to protect individuals' rights.

Conclusion

AI presents both incredible opportunities and significant ethical challenges. While the technology has the potential to improve efficiency, decision-making, and innovation, it also raises important questions about fairness, transparency, and privacy. Real-world examples like biased hiring algorithms and the misuse of facial recognition technology illustrate the risks of unchecked AI development.

Human oversight, transparency, and accountability are essential in ensuring that AI is developed and used ethically. By implementing robust auditing processes, involving human decision-makers in critical areas, and adopting ethical AI frameworks, we can harness the power of AI while minimizing harm and protecting individuals' rights.

As AI continues to evolve and play an increasingly prominent role in society, it is crucial that we address these ethical concerns and ensure that AI is developed for the benefit of all, not just a select few.

CHAPTER 13: THE FUTURE OF WORK: AI AND JOB AUTOMATION

As artificial intelligence (AI) continues to evolve, it is reshaping the future of work by automating tasks and transforming entire industries. While AI offers significant benefits in terms of efficiency and productivity, it also raises questions about the future of employment, job displacement, and how workers can adapt to this changing landscape. In this chapter, we will explore how AI is automating tasks across various industries, examine the sectors most affected by AI-driven automation, and look at real-world examples like AI in customer service (chatbots) and warehouse robots.

How AI is Changing the Job Market and Automating Tasks

AI is rapidly altering the job market by automating a wide range of tasks, from simple, repetitive duties to more complex, cognitive functions. Automation driven by AI and machine learning allows companies to improve efficiency, reduce costs, and scale their operations, but it also has implications for the workforce.

The Rise of AI-Driven Automation

Automation is not a new phenomenon, but AI has taken it to the next level by enabling machines to perform tasks that previously required human intelligence. AI systems can process large volumes of data, identify patterns, and make decisions faster and more accurately than humans. This allows companies to automate tasks in areas such as manufacturing, logistics, customer service, and even knowledge-based work.

Task Automation Across Different Levels:

1. **Repetitive manual tasks**: These are the first to be automated by AI. For instance, data entry, basic calculations, and assembly line tasks are increasingly being performed by AI-powered robots or software systems.

2. **Cognitive tasks**: AI is now automating more complex tasks that involve decision-making, pattern recognition, and even some forms of creativity. This includes things like analyzing customer behavior for personalized marketing, processing legal documents for review, and generating reports from data.

3. **Human interaction tasks**: AI has advanced to the point where it can handle certain customer-facing tasks that previously required human interaction. This includes customer service chatbots, virtual assistants, and AI-driven sales and marketing tools that can engage with customers in real time.

Benefits and Challenges of AI Automation

AI-driven automation offers several benefits, including increased productivity, reduced operational costs, and the ability to scale operations more efficiently. However, it also presents challenges, particularly in terms of **job displacement**. While AI can enhance human productivity by automating repetitive tasks, it also raises concerns about the potential for job loss in certain sectors.

- **Increased productivity**: Automation allows businesses to process tasks more quickly, leading to increased output and reduced errors. In industries like manufacturing and logistics, this can lead to faster production times and more efficient supply chain management.

- **Job displacement**: The automation of routine tasks may lead to the displacement of certain jobs, particularly in sectors like manufacturing, transportation, and customer service. Workers in these industries may need to upskill or transition into new roles that require more complex, non-automatable tasks.

- **Job transformation**: Rather than eliminating jobs, AI is transforming many roles by augmenting human workers with AI-powered tools. In many cases, workers are shifting from task-based roles to ones that require critical thinking, creativity, and the ability to collaborate with AI systems.

Industries Most Affected by AI-Driven Automation

While AI has the potential to impact all industries, certain sectors are more vulnerable to automation due to the nature of the tasks involved. Industries that rely heavily on repetitive tasks, data processing, and logistics are already seeing significant automation, while more creative and complex roles are still largely driven by human expertise.

1. Manufacturing

Manufacturing has long been a sector where automation has played a significant role, but AI is taking it further by enabling more advanced, flexible, and efficient processes. AI-driven **robots** are being used to perform complex tasks that require precision, speed, and consistency, such as assembling electronics, welding car parts, or packaging goods.

Key Examples:

- **Industrial robots**: AI-powered robots are increasingly used in factories to automate tasks such as assembly, quality control, and packaging. Unlike traditional manufacturing robots, which are programmed to perform specific tasks, AI robots can adapt to changes in their environment and learn from new data.
- **Predictive maintenance**: AI is also being used in predictive maintenance, where sensors collect data from machines and use AI algorithms to predict when equipment is likely to fail. This allows companies to perform maintenance before a breakdown occurs, reducing downtime and saving costs.

Impact on Jobs:

Manufacturing jobs that involve routine, repetitive tasks are at high risk of automation. However, AI has also created new roles in manufacturing, such as **robot technicians**, **data analysts**, and **AI system managers**, who ensure that automated systems run efficiently.

2. Logistics and Supply Chain Management

AI is revolutionizing logistics and supply chain management by improving route planning, warehouse operations, and inventory management. AI systems can analyze massive amounts of data in real time to optimize delivery routes, reduce transportation costs, and ensure timely deliveries.

Key Examples:

- **Autonomous vehicles**: AI is driving innovation in **self-driving trucks** and delivery vehicles, which can transport goods without human intervention. Companies like **Waymo** and **Tesla** are developing autonomous trucks that can make long-distance deliveries more efficiently and safely.
- **Smart warehouses**: AI-driven robots are being used in warehouses to automate tasks like picking, packing, and sorting products. These robots can work around the clock, reducing labor costs and increasing throughput.

Impact on Jobs:

Jobs in logistics, particularly those related to driving and warehouse operations, are at high risk of being automated. However, as with manufacturing, AI is also creating new roles in areas like fleet management, AI system maintenance, and logistics planning.

3. Customer Service

AI is significantly transforming customer service by automating interactions through **chatbots**, **virtual assistants**, and **AI-driven support systems**. These systems can handle a wide range of customer queries, from answering basic questions to resolving more complex issues, reducing the need for human agents.

Key Examples:

- **Chatbots**: AI-powered chatbots, like those used by companies such as **H&M** and **LivePerson**, can engage with customers in real time to answer questions, process orders, and resolve issues. Chatbots can handle high volumes of queries simultaneously, providing 24/7 support at a fraction of the cost of human agents.
- **Virtual assistants**: Virtual assistants, such as **Amazon's Alexa** and **Google Assistant**, are being used not only in customer service but also in retail and banking to provide personalized recommendations and assist with transactions.

Impact on Jobs:

Customer service roles, particularly those involving routine tasks like answering common questions or processing orders, are increasingly being automated by AI. However, human agents are still necessary for handling more complex issues, and AI systems are being used to support human workers by automating repetitive tasks, allowing them to focus on higher-value interactions.

4. Retail

The retail industry is also being transformed by AI, with automation impacting everything from inventory management to customer interactions. **AI-driven recommendation engines** personalize the shopping experience for customers, while **smart shelves** and **self-checkout systems** streamline the shopping process.

Key Examples:

- **Inventory management**: AI systems can predict demand for products, helping retailers optimize their inventory levels and reduce waste. By analyzing sales trends, weather patterns, and consumer behavior, AI can ensure that the right products are available when needed.

- **Automated checkout**: AI is powering automated checkout systems, where customers can scan and pay for items without needing to interact with a cashier. Amazon's **Just Walk Out** technology, used in its **Amazon Go** stores, allows customers to walk out with their purchases while AI tracks what they've taken and charges them automatically.

Impact on Jobs:

Roles like cashiers and stock clerks are increasingly being automated by AI systems. However, AI is also creating opportunities in areas like data analysis, inventory management, and customer experience design, where humans work alongside AI to improve retail operations.

Real-World Example: AI in Customer Service Automation and Warehouse Robots

AI in Customer Service: Chatbots and Virtual Assistants

One of the most widespread applications of AI-driven automation is in **customer service**, where chatbots and virtual assistants are transforming the way businesses interact with customers.

Case Study: H&M's AI Chatbot

Fashion retailer **H&M** uses an AI-powered chatbot to assist customers with a wide range of tasks, from finding products to tracking orders. The chatbot uses natural language processing (NLP) to understand customer inquiries and provide accurate responses in real time. By automating routine customer service interactions, H&M's chatbot reduces the need for human agents and allows the company to provide 24/7 support to customers.

- **Benefits**: H&M's chatbot can handle thousands of inquiries simultaneously, improving response times and customer satisfaction. It also reduces operational costs by reducing the number of human agents needed for basic tasks.

- **Challenges**: While the chatbot is effective at handling routine queries, more complex issues still require human intervention. H&M uses a hybrid approach, where chatbots handle the initial interaction and escalate more challenging problems to human agents.

AI in Warehouses: Robotics and Automation

In the logistics and retail industries, **warehouse robots** are playing a crucial role in automating tasks such as picking, packing, and sorting products. AI-powered robots are capable of navigating complex warehouse environments and performing repetitive tasks with speed and precision.

Case Study: Amazon's Robotics in Fulfillment Centers

Amazon has been a leader in warehouse automation, using **Kiva robots** (now called **Amazon Robotics**) to automate much of the work in its fulfillment centers. These robots move products from storage to packing stations, where human workers then prepare the items for shipment. The AI behind these robots allows them to optimize their movements, reducing the time it takes to fulfill an order and minimizing errors.

- **Benefits**: By automating the movement of products, Amazon has significantly increased the efficiency of its warehouses, allowing the company to fulfill orders more quickly and meet high customer demand, particularly during peak shopping seasons.

- **Challenges**: While Amazon's robots have automated many tasks, human workers are still required for tasks like packing, quality control, and managing complex orders. The introduction of robotics has also raised concerns about worker displacement and the need for new skill sets in a highly automated environment.

Conclusion

AI and automation are reshaping the future of work, bringing both opportunities and challenges for businesses and workers alike. While AI can improve efficiency and reduce operational costs, it also raises concerns about job displacement and the need for workers to adapt to a rapidly changing job market. Industries such as manufacturing, logistics, customer service, and retail are seeing significant impacts from AI-driven automation, with many routine tasks being automated by robots, chatbots, and AI systems.

However, AI is not just eliminating jobs—it is also creating new roles that require skills in data analysis, AI system management, and human-AI collaboration. As AI continues to advance, workers will need to upskill and transition into roles that complement AI, while businesses will need to find ways to balance automation with the human touch that remains essential in many industries.

CHAPTER 14: AI IN CREATIVITY: CAN MACHINES BE ARTISTS?

For centuries, creativity has been considered a uniquely human trait, encompassing our ability to produce art, music, literature, and other forms of expression that evoke emotion and communicate ideas. However, with the rapid development of artificial intelligence (AI), this notion is being challenged. AI systems are now capable of generating music, painting artwork, writing poetry, and even crafting entire novels. In this chapter, we will explore AI's role in creative industries, from producing AI-generated art and music to writing stories. We'll look at real-world examples such as **Google's DeepDream** and **OpenAI's GPT-3**, and consider what the future holds for AI in the realm of creativity.

AI's Role in Creative Industries: Art, Music, and Literature

AI has made inroads into the creative industries, where it is being used to assist, collaborate, and even lead the creative process. While AI is not capable of the human experience that often drives creativity—such as emotion, culture, or personal inspiration—it is proving to be a powerful tool for artists, musicians, and writers.

1. AI in Visual Art

AI's ability to generate visual art has attracted significant attention, especially with the rise of **neural networks** and **deep learning**.

These technologies allow AI systems to analyze and replicate artistic styles, generate new compositions, and even create entirely novel artwork that blends multiple styles together.

AI-Generated Art

One of the most famous examples of AI-generated art is **Google's DeepDream**, a neural network designed to enhance and distort images in surreal and psychedelic ways. Initially developed to visualize how neural networks interpret images, DeepDream became a creative tool in its own right, generating fantastical, dream-like images that captivated both the art world and the public.

- **How DeepDream Works**: DeepDream is built on a convolutional neural network (CNN) trained to recognize objects in images. By feeding an image through the network and amplifying the patterns it recognizes, DeepDream generates hallucinatory visuals, often filled with bizarre shapes, colors, and textures.

- **Artistic Impact**: While DeepDream wasn't initially intended for artistic purposes, it quickly gained popularity as a tool for creating unique digital art. The software's ability to "dream" by enhancing visual features sparked discussions about the intersection of technology and creativity. DeepDream-inspired art has been exhibited in galleries, used in music videos, and incorporated into various digital art projects.

AI-Assisted Creativity

AI is also being used to assist human artists by analyzing existing works and suggesting creative enhancements. **Style transfer**, a technique that allows AI to apply the visual style of one artwork to another, is an example of how AI can collaborate with artists to generate new creations. This technique has been applied in apps like **Prisma**, which transforms users' photos into stylized images based on the works of famous painters like Van Gogh or Picasso.

- **Example**: Artists can use AI tools like **DeepArt.io** to upload an image and choose a specific art style, allowing the algorithm to reimagine the image in that style. This enables artists to experiment with different aesthetics, blending AI-driven style transfer with their own creative intent.

2. AI in Music

AI's role in music is growing, with machine learning algorithms capable of composing melodies, generating harmonies, and even producing full tracks in various genres. AI systems are trained on vast datasets of existing music, learning the patterns, structures, and rhythms that define different styles and genres.

AI-Composed Music

One of the most well-known AI systems for generating music is **OpenAI's MuseNet**, a deep learning model capable of composing complex, multi-instrumental music in a range of styles, from classical to jazz to pop.

- **How MuseNet Works**: MuseNet is trained on a dataset of MIDI files, which represent musical compositions in a format that can be easily analyzed by computers. The AI model learns the patterns and relationships between notes, chords, and instruments, allowing it to compose new pieces that mimic the structure and style of human-created music.

- **Real-World Application**: AI-generated music has been used in video games, film scores, and as background music for various applications. For instance, companies like **Aiva Technologies** offer AI-generated music tailored for advertisements, corporate videos, and digital content. Aiva's AI system composes music based on user input, such as the desired mood or genre, allowing creators to quickly generate original scores.

AI as a Creative Partner in Music

Rather than replacing human composers, AI is often seen as a **creative partner**, augmenting the capabilities of musicians and providing them with new tools for experimentation. AI can assist musicians in generating ideas, suggesting harmonies, or even remixing existing tracks in innovative ways.

- **Example**: The band **YACHT** used AI to create their album "Chain Tripping" by training machine learning models on their previous discography. The AI-generated melodies and lyrics served as the foundation for the band's creative process, which they then refined and transformed into the final tracks.

3. AI in Literature

AI's ability to generate text has led to advancements in creative writing, including poetry, stories, and even full-length novels. **Natural language processing (NLP)** models like **OpenAI's GPT-3** are capable of producing human-like text, writing anything from essays to dialogue to short stories.

GPT-3: The Writer AI

OpenAI's **GPT-3** is one of the most advanced language models ever created, capable of generating coherent, contextually relevant text based on a given prompt. GPT-3's versatility has made it a popular tool for both professional writers and hobbyists looking to explore AI-assisted storytelling.

- **How GPT-3 Works**: GPT-3 is a transformer-based model trained on vast amounts of text from the internet, books, and articles. By learning the structure and meaning of language, GPT-3 can generate original text that mimics the style and tone of human writing.

- **Real-World Use**: GPT-3 has been used to generate poetry, blog posts, and even short stories. In one example, GPT-3 was tasked with writing a novel based on a prompt, and while the result wasn't perfect, it demonstrated the model's potential for generating creative content. Writers have also used GPT-3 to overcome writer's block, generating ideas or exploring new narrative directions.

AI and Poetry

AI-generated poetry is another area where AI is beginning to have an impact. While poetry is often seen as deeply personal and emotional, AI systems can create poems that adhere to traditional forms, rhyme schemes, and meter.

- **Example**: AI-generated poems have been exhibited in galleries and even featured in literary journals. In some cases, poets collaborate with AI by inputting specific themes or styles, allowing the AI to generate verses that the poet can refine and incorporate into their own work.

Real-World Examples: AI-Generated Music and Art

Several high-profile examples of AI-generated music and art have captured the public's imagination and demonstrated the creative potential of AI. Let's look at two of the most prominent examples—

Google DeepDream and **OpenAI's GPT-3**—and how they are pushing the boundaries of creativity.

1. Google DeepDream: Surreal AI Art

As mentioned earlier, **DeepDream** was developed by researchers at Google to visualize how deep neural networks interpret images. While its primary purpose was to analyze the internal workings of AI models, DeepDream quickly became a creative tool for artists interested in exploring the intersection of technology and imagination.

- **DeepDream's impact**: The bizarre, dream-like images produced by DeepDream have inspired artists to incorporate AI-generated elements into their work. In some cases, DeepDream has been used to create large-scale digital artworks, and its distinctive style has become a recognizable aesthetic in AI art.
- **Artistic collaborations**: DeepDream has also led to collaborations between human artists and AI, with artists using the tool to enhance or transform their existing work. This blending of human creativity and machine-generated output highlights the potential of AI to act as a creative partner in visual arts.

2. OpenAI's GPT-3: AI in Writing and Storytelling

GPT-3 has become one of the most talked-about AI systems due to its remarkable ability to generate human-like text. It has been used in various creative writing projects, from generating poetry to crafting entire narratives.

- **Example: AI-generated stories**: GPT-3 has been used by writers to create short stories and novels, offering a glimpse into what AI-generated literature might look like in the future. By feeding the AI a prompt or a few lines of text, writers can explore the different directions GPT-3 takes their stories, often generating surprising and creative results.

- **GPT-3 in journalism and content creation**: Beyond literature, GPT-3 is also being used in journalism, where it can generate news summaries, blog posts, and articles. In some cases, GPT-3's writing is nearly indistinguishable from that of a human writer, raising questions about the future of content creation and the role of AI in media.

The Future of AI in Creative Fields

As AI continues to evolve, its role in creative fields is likely to expand. The technology will increasingly be used to assist and augment human creativity, pushing the boundaries of what artists, musicians, and writers can achieve.

1. AI as a Creative Tool

Rather than replacing human creativity, AI is more likely to be viewed as a tool that enhances and complements human efforts. By automating certain aspects of the creative process, such as generating ideas or suggesting modifications, AI can free artists to focus on higher-level conceptual work.

- **Human-AI collaboration**: In the future, we may see more collaborations between human creators and AI systems, with AI acting as a creative partner that provides new perspectives and possibilities. This collaboration could lead to entirely new genres of art, music, and literature that blend human imagination with machine learning.

2. Democratizing Creativity

AI's ability to generate art, music, and literature also has the potential to **democratize creativity**, making it more accessible to people who may not have formal training in these fields. With AI tools, individuals can create professional-quality artwork, compose music, or write stories without needing to master the technical skills traditionally required.

- **Creative apps and tools**: As AI-powered creative tools become more sophisticated, we can expect to see an increase in apps and platforms that allow users to generate art or music with minimal effort. These tools will make creativity more inclusive, allowing anyone with access to AI technology to express themselves artistically.

3. Ethical Considerations and Copyright Issues

As AI becomes more integrated into creative fields, it raises important ethical questions about **authorship** and **copyright**. If an AI system generates a piece of art or music, who owns the copyright?

Should the human who trained or directed the AI be credited as the artist, or is the AI itself the creator?

- **Copyright laws**: Current copyright laws are not well-equipped to handle AI-generated content, and there are ongoing debates about how intellectual property rights should be assigned in cases where AI plays a significant role in the creative process.

- **Authenticity and originality**: There is also the question of what constitutes originality in AI-generated work. While AI can generate new content, it often does so by analyzing and replicating existing works, raising questions about the authenticity of AI-generated creations.

Conclusion

AI is challenging traditional notions of creativity by enabling machines to produce art, music, and literature that, in some cases, rivals human output. From Google's DeepDream creating surrealist visuals to OpenAI's GPT-3 writing coherent stories, AI is proving that it can be a powerful tool in the creative process. However, AI is not a replacement for human creativity—it is a collaborator, capable of generating new possibilities while leaving the final vision and direction in human hands.

As AI continues to evolve, its role in creative fields will likely grow, providing artists, musicians, and writers with new ways to express themselves and pushing the boundaries of what is possible. However, the rise of AI-generated content also raises important ethical questions about authorship, copyright, and the definition of creativity itself.

CHAPTER 15: REINFORCEMENT LEARNING: TEACHING AI THROUGH REWARDS

Reinforcement learning (RL) is one of the most fascinating and powerful approaches to artificial intelligence (AI). In contrast to other types of machine learning, where AI is trained on labeled data or predefined rules, reinforcement learning allows AI to learn through experience by interacting with its environment and receiving feedback in the form of rewards or penalties. This chapter will explore the concept of reinforcement learning in simplified terms, explain how it's used to train AI to perform complex tasks, and examine real-world examples, including **AlphaGo**, the AI system that mastered the ancient game of Go.

Simplified Explanation of Reinforcement Learning

At its core, **reinforcement learning** (RL) is a framework for teaching AI by simulating how humans and animals learn from their environment. It is inspired by the idea that we often learn through trial and error, making decisions based on feedback from our actions. In RL, an AI agent learns by taking actions in an environment, observing the results, and adjusting its behavior based on the rewards or penalties it receives.

Key Components of Reinforcement Learning

1. **Agent**: The **agent** is the decision-maker in a reinforcement learning system—essentially, the AI itself. It interacts with the environment, observes the results of its actions, and learns from the feedback it receives.

2. **Environment**: The **environment** is everything the agent interacts with. It could be a virtual world (like a game or simulation) or a real-world scenario (like a robot moving through a room). The environment provides feedback to the agent in the form of rewards or penalties.

3. **Action**: An **action** is any decision or move made by the agent. Actions are the steps the agent takes to achieve a goal, such as moving a piece on a game board or navigating through a maze.

4. **State**: The **state** represents the current situation or condition of the environment that the agent can observe. For example, in a chess game, the state would be the arrangement of pieces on the board.

5. **Reward**: The **reward** is feedback provided to the agent after it takes an action. Rewards can be positive (reinforcing good behavior) or negative (discouraging bad behavior). The goal of the agent is to maximize the cumulative reward it receives over time.

6. **Policy**: A **policy** is the strategy or set of rules that the agent follows when deciding which actions to take. Over time, the agent refines its policy to maximize its rewards.

The Learning Process in Reinforcement Learning

Reinforcement learning operates through a cycle of **trial and error**:

1. **The agent takes an action** in its environment based on its current policy.
2. The environment **responds to that action**, producing a new state and giving the agent a reward (or penalty).
3. The agent **learns** from this experience by adjusting its policy to increase the likelihood of receiving more rewards in the future.

Over time, the agent improves its performance by learning which actions lead to positive outcomes and which ones lead to negative outcomes. The agent may start with random actions but gradually refines its behavior as it accumulates experience.

How Reinforcement Learning is Used to Train AI in Complex Tasks

Reinforcement learning is particularly useful for training AI to handle **complex, sequential decision-making** tasks, where the consequences of actions are not immediately clear. This approach is well-suited for problems where an agent needs to develop a strategy, explore a large number of possible states, and make decisions in real-time. Examples of such tasks include playing games, controlling robots, optimizing systems, and managing resources.

1. Games and Strategy Development

One of the most well-known applications of reinforcement learning is in **games**, where AI agents must develop complex strategies to outsmart opponents. Games provide a structured environment with clear rules, states, and rewards, making them an ideal testing ground for reinforcement learning algorithms.

AlphaGo and DeepMind's Breakthrough

Perhaps the most famous example of reinforcement learning in action is **AlphaGo**, an AI system developed by **DeepMind**, a subsidiary of Google. AlphaGo made headlines in 2016 when it defeated the world champion **Lee Sedol** in the ancient board game of **Go**, a game known for its extraordinary complexity and vast number of possible moves.

- **Why Go is Challenging**: Go is much more complex than games like chess. While chess has about 10^{120} possible moves, Go has an astronomical 10^{170} possible board configurations. This makes it nearly impossible for traditional AI methods, which rely on brute-force search, to effectively play Go at a high level. Instead, AlphaGo used reinforcement learning to master the game.

- **How AlphaGo Learned**: AlphaGo's training began by learning from millions of past games played by human Go players. However, the real breakthrough came when AlphaGo started playing games against itself, using reinforcement learning to refine its strategies. By continuously adjusting its policy based on the rewards it received for winning games, AlphaGo gradually became one of the most skilled Go players in the world.

- **Policy and Value Networks**: AlphaGo's architecture consisted of two key components: a **policy network** that helped it decide which moves to play and a **value network** that evaluated the current state of the game to estimate the likelihood of winning. These neural networks worked together to allow AlphaGo to anticipate the long-term consequences of its actions and make highly strategic decisions.

AlphaGo's success marked a major milestone in AI research, demonstrating that reinforcement learning could be used to solve problems previously thought to be too complex for machines.

2. Robotics and Physical Interaction

Reinforcement learning is also widely used in **robotics**, where robots must learn to perform physical tasks by interacting with their environment. Tasks like walking, grasping objects, or navigating through space involve real-time decision-making, requiring the robot to adapt to changing conditions and learn from trial and error.

Example: Robotic Manipulation

AI systems trained through reinforcement learning have been used to teach robots how to **manipulate objects** with greater precision. For example, a robot can be trained to pick up objects of different shapes and sizes using reinforcement learning. Initially, the robot might fail to grasp the object correctly, but over time, it learns the optimal grip by receiving rewards for successful attempts and penalties for failed ones.

- **Robotic arms**: Industrial robotic arms, such as those used in manufacturing, can be trained to perform tasks like assembly or packaging using reinforcement learning. The robots learn how much pressure to apply, how to position themselves, and how to adapt to slight variations in the objects they handle.

- **Autonomous drones**: Autonomous drones also use reinforcement learning to navigate complex environments, avoiding obstacles while optimizing their path to a destination. By exploring different flight paths and receiving rewards for successfully completing missions, drones improve their navigation capabilities.

3. Self-Driving Cars

Another area where reinforcement learning plays a crucial role is in the development of **self-driving cars**. These vehicles must navigate complex road conditions, make split-second decisions, and adapt to unpredictable situations like changing traffic patterns or unexpected obstacles. Reinforcement learning allows AI to handle these challenges by continuously learning from its environment.

How Self-Driving Cars Use Reinforcement Learning

Self-driving cars use reinforcement learning to optimize their **driving strategies**:

- **Navigating traffic**: Reinforcement learning enables the AI to learn how to navigate traffic, maintain safe distances from other vehicles, and follow traffic laws, all while minimizing travel time.

- **Avoiding collisions**: The AI receives negative rewards (penalties) when the vehicle gets too close to another car or makes unsafe maneuvers. Over time, the system learns to avoid these mistakes and improve its safety performance.

- **Real-time adaptation**: As the AI drives, it learns from the environment and adapts to real-time changes. For example, if a road is blocked or conditions are slippery due to rain, the car must adjust its driving behavior accordingly.

Tesla, Waymo, and other companies developing autonomous vehicles are using reinforcement learning in combination with other AI techniques to build cars that can safely and efficiently drive without human intervention.

Real-World Example: AlphaGo and Teaching AI to Play Games

As mentioned earlier, **AlphaGo** is one of the most iconic examples of reinforcement learning in action. But AlphaGo wasn't the only AI system to achieve mastery in complex games. AI has also excelled in games like **chess**, **poker**, and even **StarCraft**, showing the versatility of reinforcement learning in mastering complex environments.

The Success of AlphaGo

The game of Go is considered one of the ultimate tests of strategic thinking due to its complexity. Traditional AI approaches, such as brute-force search, are insufficient for Go because of the sheer number of possible moves at each step. AlphaGo's use of reinforcement learning, combined with neural networks, allowed it to go beyond human intuition and develop highly advanced strategies.

- **Learning through self-play**: After learning from human games, AlphaGo began playing games against itself, using reinforcement learning to improve. Each time AlphaGo played a game, it received rewards for winning and penalties for losing. By analyzing the results of each match, AlphaGo refined its strategies and learned to avoid moves that led to losses while favoring those that increased its chances of winning.

- **Victory against world champion**: In March 2016, AlphaGo defeated **Lee Sedol**, a world champion Go player, in a historic five-game match. The victory stunned the AI and Go communities, as many had believed that it would take decades for AI to match the skill level of top human Go players.

- **Beyond AlphaGo: AlphaZero**: Following the success of AlphaGo, DeepMind developed **AlphaZero**, a more general AI system that used reinforcement learning to master a variety of games, including Go, chess, and shogi. AlphaZero was not trained on human games but learned entirely through self-play, further demonstrating the power of reinforcement learning in mastering complex tasks without human input.

Reinforcement Learning in Chess and StarCraft

In addition to Go, reinforcement learning has been used to train AI systems to play other challenging games:

- **Chess**: AlphaZero also became one of the world's strongest chess players by learning to play the game from scratch. Without any prior knowledge or training on human chess games, AlphaZero mastered the game in a matter of hours, using reinforcement learning to develop novel strategies that even surprised grandmasters.

- **StarCraft**: In 2019, DeepMind's **AlphaStar** became the first AI to defeat professional human players in the real-time strategy game **StarCraft II**. Reinforcement learning allowed AlphaStar to learn complex strategies involving resource management, unit control, and long-term planning in a dynamic and fast-paced environment.

The Future of Reinforcement Learning

As reinforcement learning continues to evolve, its applications will extend beyond games and robotics into new areas such as healthcare, finance, and personalized education.

1. Healthcare

Reinforcement learning has the potential to revolutionize healthcare by optimizing treatment plans, improving drug discovery, and enhancing medical diagnostics.

- **Personalized treatment**: In healthcare, reinforcement learning could be used to create personalized treatment plans for patients. By analyzing patient data and continuously learning from the outcomes of different treatments, AI systems could recommend the best course of action for managing chronic conditions or optimizing medication dosages.

- **Robotic surgery**: Reinforcement learning could also improve robotic surgery by allowing AI systems to learn from surgical procedures and refine their techniques over time. This could lead to more precise and less invasive surgeries with improved outcomes for patients.

2. Finance

Reinforcement learning is already being applied in the financial industry to optimize trading strategies, manage portfolios, and predict market trends.

- **Automated trading**: AI-driven trading systems use reinforcement learning to explore different investment strategies and maximize returns. By continuously learning from market conditions, these systems can adapt their trading decisions to changing economic environments.
- **Risk management**: Reinforcement learning can help financial institutions optimize risk management by analyzing large datasets and predicting potential risks, such as credit defaults or market crashes.

3. Education

In education, reinforcement learning could be used to create personalized learning experiences for students.

- **Adaptive learning**: AI-driven learning platforms could use reinforcement learning to adjust the difficulty and content of lessons based on a student's performance. By providing real-time feedback and rewards, these systems could motivate students to stay engaged and improve their understanding of subjects over time.

Conclusion

Reinforcement learning is a powerful method for teaching AI to solve complex problems by learning from its actions and the feedback it receives from the environment. From mastering games like Go and chess to controlling robots and self-driving cars, reinforcement learning allows AI to develop sophisticated strategies and adapt to new challenges. Real-world successes like **AlphaGo** highlight the potential of reinforcement learning to tackle problems that were once thought to be beyond the reach of machines.

As AI continues to advance, reinforcement learning will play an increasingly important role in areas such as healthcare, finance, and education. By enabling AI to learn through trial and error, reinforcement learning provides a flexible and scalable approach to solving complex tasks, offering new possibilities for the future of AI and its impact on society.

CHAPTER 16: THE HARDWARE BEHIND AI: GPUS, TPUS, AND MORE

While much of the focus on artificial intelligence (AI) revolves around algorithms, models, and data, the hardware that powers AI is equally critical. The growing complexity of machine learning and deep learning tasks requires immense computational power, which traditional computer processors (CPUs) are often unable to provide efficiently. Specialized hardware, such as **Graphics Processing Units (GPUs)** and **Tensor Processing Units (TPUs)**, has emerged as a key enabler of AI's rapid advancement. In this chapter, we'll explore the hardware behind AI and machine learning, look at **Nvidia's GPUs** as a real-world example, and discuss the role of **cloud computing** in AI development.

What Kind of Hardware Powers AI and Machine Learning?

Training AI models—especially deep learning models—requires performing vast amounts of complex mathematical calculations. Traditional **CPUs** (Central Processing Units), while versatile, are often too slow for the parallel processing tasks required by AI, particularly for large-scale deep learning projects that involve enormous datasets and extensive matrix calculations. As AI has grown more demanding, specialized hardware has emerged to meet the computational needs of AI models.

1. Graphics Processing Units (GPUs)

GPUs were originally designed to accelerate the rendering of images and graphics for video games and other visual applications. Unlike CPUs, which are optimized for sequential processing, GPUs excel at **parallel processing**—performing many calculations simultaneously. This makes them ideal for the kinds of matrix and vector operations that are common in machine learning and deep learning algorithms.

Why GPUs are Essential for AI

GPUs are essential for training deep learning models, particularly when dealing with neural networks, which require billions of operations to adjust weights and biases across multiple layers.

- **Parallel Processing**: The ability to perform thousands of calculations in parallel allows GPUs to dramatically speed up the training of machine learning models. While a CPU might have a few dozen cores, a GPU can have thousands, making it much more efficient at handling the computations involved in tasks like image recognition, language translation, and game playing.

- **Deep Learning**: Deep learning frameworks like **TensorFlow**, **PyTorch**, and **Keras** rely heavily on GPUs to process the vast amounts of data required for training models. In tasks like image classification or natural language processing (NLP), each layer of the neural network performs a large number of matrix operations, and GPUs are specifically designed to handle such operations quickly and efficiently.

- **Scalability**: GPUs allow AI researchers and developers to train models faster and with larger datasets. This scalability is key to making breakthroughs in AI, as larger models trained on more data often yield better results. For example, cutting-edge models like **GPT-3** and **AlphaGo** could not have been trained without the computational power provided by GPUs.

2. Tensor Processing Units (TPUs)

In response to the growing demands of AI, **Google** developed a specialized processor called the **Tensor Processing Unit (TPU)**. TPUs are custom-built chips designed specifically to accelerate **TensorFlow** workloads, focusing on deep learning tasks.

How TPUs Differ from GPUs

While both TPUs and GPUs are designed for high-performance parallel computing, TPUs are optimized specifically for the types of operations found in deep learning. This includes tasks like matrix multiplications, which are central to neural networks, and inference workloads, where trained models are used to make predictions based on new data.

- **Efficiency in AI Workloads**: TPUs are highly optimized for AI tasks like training large-scale models and running real-time inference. Google designed TPUs to handle TensorFlow workloads more efficiently than GPUs, especially when it comes to matrix operations.

- **Energy Efficiency**: TPUs are designed to be more energy-efficient than GPUs, which can consume a lot of power when running large AI models. This makes TPUs an attractive option for companies looking to balance performance with energy usage, particularly in large-scale AI deployments.

- **Cloud Integration**: TPUs are integrated into **Google Cloud**, providing AI researchers and developers with access to this specialized hardware through the cloud. This allows companies to scale their AI projects without needing to invest in expensive on-premise hardware.

3. Field-Programmable Gate Arrays (FPGAs)

FPGAs are another type of hardware used in AI, offering flexibility and customization. Unlike GPUs and TPUs, which are designed for specific tasks, FPGAs can be programmed to perform a wide range of operations, making them ideal for tasks that require custom hardware configurations.

- **Reprogrammability**: FPGAs can be reprogrammed after they are manufactured, allowing them to be customized for specific AI tasks. This makes them useful in applications where developers need to fine-tune the hardware to achieve the best performance for a particular algorithm or workload.

- **Low Latency**: FPGAs offer low latency, making them ideal for real-time AI applications, such as autonomous vehicles, robotics, and financial trading, where decisions need to be made in milliseconds.

Real-World Example: Nvidia's GPUs and Their Role in Accelerating AI Computation

When it comes to the hardware driving AI, **Nvidia** is one of the most prominent names in the industry. Nvidia's **GPUs** have been instrumental in the rapid progress of AI and deep learning, and the company has developed a range of products specifically designed for AI workloads.

Nvidia's Role in AI Development

Nvidia originally developed GPUs for gaming and visual computing, but it quickly became apparent that GPUs were also ideal for AI tasks, particularly deep learning. The company's GPUs are now used in everything from academic research to large-scale AI deployments in industries such as healthcare, automotive, and finance.

CUDA: Nvidia's Parallel Computing Platform

A key component of Nvidia's success in AI is its **CUDA (Compute Unified Device Architecture)** platform, which allows developers to harness the parallel computing power of GPUs for general-purpose computing tasks, including AI and machine learning.

- **Why CUDA Matters**: CUDA provides a flexible and powerful programming environment that makes it easier for developers to implement machine learning algorithms on Nvidia GPUs. This has been a game-changer for AI researchers, allowing them to speed up the training and execution of deep learning models.

- **Integration with AI Frameworks**: CUDA is integrated with popular deep learning frameworks like TensorFlow, PyTorch, and Caffe, enabling seamless use of GPUs to accelerate AI workloads. Nvidia's hardware and software ecosystem has made it the go-to choice for training complex AI models.

Nvidia GPUs for AI: From Research to Industry

Nvidia's GPUs are used in many industries to power AI-driven applications:

- **Healthcare**: Nvidia GPUs are used in medical imaging and diagnostics, helping AI models quickly analyze images like MRIs and CT scans to detect abnormalities or diseases. This allows doctors to make faster, more accurate diagnoses.

- **Autonomous Vehicles**: Nvidia's **DRIVE** platform provides the computing power for autonomous vehicles. Using GPUs, self-driving cars can process massive amounts of data from sensors, cameras, and LIDAR systems to make real-time decisions about navigation, obstacle avoidance, and road safety.

- **AI Research**: Many breakthroughs in AI research, such as **AlphaGo** and **GPT-3**, have been powered by Nvidia GPUs. These GPUs enable researchers to train increasingly larger models, pushing the boundaries of what AI can achieve.

Example: Nvidia A100 GPU

Nvidia's **A100 Tensor Core GPU** is one of the most advanced GPUs designed specifically for AI workloads. It is optimized for both training and inference, making it versatile enough to handle the entire AI pipeline.

- **Performance**: The A100 delivers up to 20 times the performance of previous-generation GPUs, making it capable of handling massive datasets and complex models in a fraction of the time.
- **Scalability**: The A100 can scale from single-node workloads to multi-node distributed AI training, allowing companies to train models that require massive computational resources, such as natural language processing models or large-scale image recognition systems.

The Importance of Cloud Computing in AI Development

While specialized hardware like GPUs and TPUs is crucial for AI development, not every organization has the resources to purchase and maintain expensive hardware on-premises. This is where **cloud computing** plays a pivotal role in democratizing access to AI capabilities. Cloud providers offer scalable infrastructure that enables companies and researchers to develop and deploy AI models without needing to invest in costly physical hardware.

Benefits of Cloud Computing for AI

1. **Scalability**: Cloud platforms like **Amazon Web Services (AWS)**, **Google Cloud**, and **Microsoft Azure** offer scalable resources, allowing AI developers to quickly spin up GPU or TPU instances on demand. This is especially important for AI projects that require large-scale training on massive datasets.

2. **Cost-Efficiency**: Cloud computing eliminates the need for upfront investments in hardware. Instead of purchasing expensive GPUs or TPUs, developers can rent access to these resources on a pay-as-you-go basis, reducing costs and allowing smaller organizations to experiment with AI.

3. **Flexibility**: Cloud platforms provide flexibility by offering different types of hardware, such as CPUs, GPUs, and TPUs, tailored to the specific needs of the AI model being trained.

This enables developers to choose the right infrastructure for their project.

4. **Collaboration and Accessibility**: Cloud platforms make it easier for AI teams to collaborate on projects, sharing data and models across locations. This is particularly important for large-scale AI research projects that require coordination across multiple teams and institutions.

Real-World Cloud AI Platforms

- **Google Cloud**: Google Cloud offers **AI Platform**, which provides access to TPUs and GPUs, making it easy for developers to train and deploy machine learning models at scale. Google Cloud also offers **AutoML**, which allows users to build and train custom machine learning models without needing extensive knowledge of coding or machine learning techniques.

- **AWS**: Amazon Web Services (AWS) offers **Amazon SageMaker**, a fully managed service that enables developers to build, train, and deploy machine learning models quickly. AWS provides access to GPUs, as well as specialized machine learning instances like **Inf1**, which are optimized for AI inference workloads.

- **Microsoft Azure**: Azure provides a comprehensive suite of AI tools, including **Azure Machine Learning**, which integrates with Nvidia GPUs and offers access to powerful compute resources for AI training and inference.

Hybrid AI: Combining On-Premises and Cloud Solutions

While cloud computing is highly flexible, some organizations may prefer to use **hybrid AI** solutions, combining on-premises hardware with cloud-based infrastructure. This allows businesses to run their most critical workloads locally for increased control and security, while offloading more demanding or experimental tasks to the cloud.

- **Example**: A financial services company might use on-premises Nvidia GPUs for sensitive data processing, while using cloud-based GPUs to train large AI models that require significant computational power.

Conclusion

AI's rapid progress would not be possible without the specialized hardware that powers machine learning and deep learning models. **GPUs**, **TPUs**, and other hardware accelerators have become essential tools for training AI systems to handle complex tasks. **Nvidia's GPUs**, in particular, have revolutionized the AI landscape by providing the computational power needed to train sophisticated models, from self-driving cars to medical imaging systems.

Cloud computing has also played a crucial role in democratizing access to AI hardware, allowing organizations of all sizes to experiment with AI without the need for costly infrastructure. With cloud platforms offering access to GPUs and TPUs on demand, AI development has become more scalable, flexible, and accessible than ever before.

As AI continues to evolve, we can expect hardware innovation to keep pace, driving further advancements in AI capabilities and enabling even more powerful models to tackle the world's most complex challenges.

CHAPTER 17: AI IN CYBERSECURITY: PROTECTING AGAINST DIGITAL THREATS

As technology continues to advance, so too does the complexity and frequency of cyber-attacks. Cybercriminals are becoming more sophisticated, deploying advanced techniques to steal data, disrupt services, and exploit vulnerabilities. To counter these evolving threats, artificial intelligence (AI) is being increasingly used in cybersecurity. By leveraging machine learning, pattern recognition, and real-time analysis, AI can help detect and prevent cyber-attacks more effectively than traditional methods. In this chapter, we'll explore how AI is transforming the cybersecurity landscape, look at real-world examples of AI-powered threat detection, and examine the role of AI in combating fraud and other online threats.

How AI is Used to Detect and Prevent Cyber-Attacks

The speed, scale, and complexity of modern cyber-attacks make it challenging for traditional security measures to keep up. Manual threat detection systems, which rely on human experts to analyze security data, are often too slow to identify and respond to sophisticated attacks in real-time. AI, with its ability to process vast amounts of data and detect anomalies, offers a more proactive and automated approach to cyber security.

1. AI for Threat Detection

One of the primary uses of AI in cyber security is **threat detection**. AI systems are trained to identify patterns in data that may indicate malicious activity, such as unauthorized access, data exfiltration, or system anomalies. By using machine learning algorithms, AI can detect these threats more quickly and with greater accuracy than traditional security tools.

Machine Learning for Anomaly Detection

In cyber security, **anomaly detection** refers to identifying unusual patterns or behaviors that deviate from the norm. For example, if a user typically logs into a system from a specific geographic location and suddenly attempts to log in from a distant country at an unusual time, this could be flagged as suspicious. Machine learning algorithms excel at recognizing these kinds of deviations, even when the specific nature of the attack is unknown.

- **Unsupervised learning**: AI models can use unsupervised learning to detect anomalies without relying on pre-labeled data. By learning what constitutes "normal" behavior within a network, these models can quickly flag deviations that may indicate a cyber-attack. This is particularly useful for identifying **zero-day attacks**, which exploit previously unknown vulnerabilities.

- **Behavioral analysis**: AI-based cybersecurity systems analyze user and network behaviors over time. By creating a baseline of expected activity, AI can flag deviations as potential security threats. For example, if an employee suddenly starts accessing sensitive files they've never interacted with before, this might indicate compromised credentials.

Real-Time Monitoring and Response

One of the advantages of AI in cybersecurity is its ability to operate **in real time**. AI systems can continuously monitor network traffic, user behavior, and system logs, detecting potential threats as they occur. This real-time monitoring allows for faster response times, reducing the window of opportunity for attackers to exploit vulnerabilities.

- **Automated response**: In addition to detecting threats, AI can be programmed to automatically respond to certain types of attacks. For example, if an AI system detects a Distributed Denial of Service (DDoS) attack, it can automatically reroute traffic or deploy countermeasures to mitigate the impact without needing human intervention.

2. Predictive Analytics in Cyber security

AI can also be used to predict potential attacks before they occur. By analyzing historical data on past cyber-attacks, AI models can identify patterns and indicators that suggest an attack is imminent.

This allows cybersecurity teams to take proactive measures to protect their systems.

- **Threat intelligence**: AI systems can aggregate data from a variety of sources, such as cybersecurity reports, hacker forums, and threat intelligence feeds, to predict emerging threats. This predictive capability allows organizations to strengthen their defenses before an attack happens, reducing the risk of data breaches or service disruptions.

- **Vulnerability assessment**: AI can automate vulnerability assessments, scanning systems and networks for known weaknesses. By using machine learning models that prioritize vulnerabilities based on their potential to be exploited, cyber security teams can focus on addressing the most critical risks.

Real-World Examples: AI-Powered Threat Detection in Cyber security Tools

AI is already being deployed in various cyber security tools and platforms, enabling organizations to better protect their networks and data. Let's take a look at some real-world examples of AI-powered threat detection in action.

1. Dark trace: AI for Autonomous Threat Detection

Dark trace is one of the leading companies using AI to provide **autonomous threat detection** and response for enterprises. The company's platform, powered by machine learning algorithms, is designed to detect and neutralize threats in real-time without human intervention.

How Darktrace Works

Darktrace's AI system uses **unsupervised learning** to build a detailed understanding of an organization's "normal" behavior across its digital infrastructure. Once the AI system establishes this baseline, it continuously monitors network activity for any deviations that could indicate a security threat.

- **Real-time threat detection**: Darktrace's AI can detect a wide range of cyber-attacks, including insider threats, ransomware, and data exfiltration. The system doesn't rely on pre-defined rules or signatures, making it capable of identifying novel threats and zero-day attacks that traditional security systems might miss.

- **Autonomous response**: Darktrace's **Autonomous Response** technology, known as **Antigena**, can take immediate action when it detects a threat. For example, it can automatically isolate compromised devices, block malicious communications, or slow down suspicious network activity to prevent an attack from spreading.

Real-World Impact

Darktrace's AI-powered system has been deployed across various industries, including finance, healthcare, and manufacturing. The platform has proven effective at detecting threats early, preventing data breaches, and minimizing the damage caused by cyber-attacks. By automating much of the threat detection and response process, Darktrace helps reduce the burden on human security teams while improving overall security.

2. CrowdStrike: AI in Endpoint Protection

CrowdStrike is another major player in the cybersecurity industry that uses AI to enhance endpoint protection. The company's **Falcon** platform employs AI-driven analytics to detect and prevent malware, ransomware, and other types of cyber threats targeting individual devices.

How CrowdStrike Uses AI

CrowdStrike's AI models are trained on massive datasets of malware samples, attack patterns, and cybersecurity incidents. By analyzing this data, the platform can detect threats that traditional antivirus software might miss.

- **Fileless attacks**: One of CrowdStrike's strengths is its ability to detect **fileless attacks**, where malware doesn't write files to disk but operates directly from memory. Fileless attacks are notoriously difficult to detect, but CrowdStrike's AI algorithms can identify suspicious behaviors at the endpoint level and prevent these attacks from executing.

- **Threat intelligence**: CrowdStrike's AI system also integrates with global threat intelligence feeds, allowing it to stay updated on emerging threats and adjust its defenses accordingly. This proactive approach helps reduce the risk of being caught off guard by new or evolving attack techniques.

Real-World Impact

CrowdStrike's AI-powered platform is widely used by enterprises to protect their endpoints from cyber-attacks. Its ability to detect both known and unknown threats in real-time has made it a popular choice for companies looking to safeguard their devices, networks, and data. The platform's success in detecting advanced threats has earned it a reputation as one of the most effective AI-driven cybersecurity solutions on the market.

The Role of AI in Combating Fraud and Online Threats

AI is also playing a crucial role in combating **fraud** and other types of **online threats**, such as identity theft, phishing, and financial crimes. These types of attacks often involve subtle patterns that are difficult for humans to detect, making them ideal candidates for AI-driven detection and prevention systems.

1. AI for Fraud Detection

Fraud is a major concern in sectors such as finance, e-commerce, and insurance. AI systems, particularly those based on machine learning, can analyze vast amounts of transaction data to identify fraudulent behavior in real-time.

Machine Learning for Transaction Monitoring

In the financial industry, AI-powered fraud detection systems monitor transactions for signs of suspicious activity. These systems can detect **anomalies**, such as unusually large purchases, multiple transactions from different geographic locations, or sudden changes in spending patterns, that may indicate fraudulent behavior.

- **Credit card fraud**: AI models are commonly used to detect credit card fraud by analyzing transaction patterns. When a customer makes a purchase, the AI system compares the transaction to previous behavior, flagging any activity that seems unusual. If the system identifies a potential fraud, it can automatically freeze the account or notify the customer for verification.

- **Insurance fraud**: AI is also being used in the insurance industry to detect fraudulent claims. By analyzing claim histories, accident reports, and policyholder data, AI models can identify patterns that are consistent with fraudulent claims and flag them for further investigation.

Real-World Example: PayPal

PayPal, one of the world's leading online payment platforms, uses AI and machine learning to combat fraud. PayPal processes billions of transactions each year, making it a prime target for fraudsters. The company's AI-driven fraud detection system continuously monitors transactions for unusual behavior, allowing it to block suspicious transactions in real-time.

- **Adaptive learning**: PayPal's AI system uses **adaptive learning** to adjust its fraud detection strategies as new threats emerge. The system learns from past fraud attempts, refining its models to become more effective at identifying new tactics used by cybercriminals.

2. AI in Phishing Detection

Phishing attacks are one of the most common types of cyber-attacks, where attackers trick individuals into revealing sensitive information such as passwords or credit card numbers by posing as legitimate entities. AI is increasingly being used to combat phishing by analyzing email patterns, domain names, and communication behavior to detect and block phishing attempts before they reach users.

Machine Learning for Email Filtering

AI-powered email filters can detect phishing attempts by analyzing the content and metadata of incoming emails. Machine learning models are trained to recognize common indicators of phishing, such as suspicious links, fake domain names, and misleading language.

- **Natural Language Processing (NLP)**: AI systems use **NLP** to analyze the content of emails for phishing indicators. For example, AI can detect patterns of urgency, poor grammar, or unusual requests that are common in phishing emails. The system can then flag these emails as suspicious or move them to a quarantine folder before they reach the recipient.

- **URL analysis**: AI systems also analyze URLs embedded in emails to determine if they lead to legitimate websites or malicious sites designed to steal credentials. If the AI detects a suspicious URL, it can block access to the site or warn the user.

Real-World Example: Google's AI-Powered Gmail Filters

Google uses AI to protect Gmail users from phishing attacks. Gmail's AI-powered filters analyze incoming emails for signs of phishing and malware. According to Google, the system blocks more than **100 million phishing emails** each day.

- **Advanced threat detection**: Google's AI system uses machine learning to continuously improve its ability to detect phishing attempts. As phishing tactics evolve, the AI models learn from new threats, ensuring that users remain protected against the latest scams.

The Future of AI in Cybersecurity

As cyber-attacks become more sophisticated, the role of AI in cybersecurity will continue to grow. AI has proven effective at detecting and preventing threats in real-time, but there are still challenges to overcome.

1. AI Arms Race: Attackers Using AI

One emerging concern is the possibility that cybercriminals will begin using AI to enhance their attacks. Just as AI can be used to detect threats, it can also be used to bypass defenses or create more advanced forms of malware. This has led to an **"AI arms race"** in cybersecurity, where both defenders and attackers are using AI to outsmart one another.

- **AI-powered malware**: Cybercriminals could use AI to develop malware that adapts to different environments, making it harder to detect. AI-powered malware could learn from its environment, changing its behavior to avoid detection by traditional security measures.
- **AI-driven social engineering**: AI could also be used to create more convincing phishing attacks or other social engineering techniques. For example, AI systems could generate personalized phishing emails that are more difficult for users to identify as fraudulent.

2. Human-AI Collaboration in Cybersecurity

Despite AI's growing capabilities, human expertise remains essential in cybersecurity. AI is most effective when combined with human analysts who can interpret the results, investigate complex threats, and make critical decisions. In the future, cybersecurity will likely involve a **collaborative approach** between human experts and AI systems, with each playing a complementary role.

- **AI for triage**: AI can automate the detection of threats and provide initial analysis, allowing human experts to focus on the most critical issues. This collaboration improves efficiency and reduces the risk of human error, while still ensuring that complex threats receive the attention of skilled security professionals.

Conclusion

AI is transforming the field of cybersecurity by providing faster, more accurate threat detection and response capabilities. Through machine learning, anomaly detection, and predictive analytics, AI-powered tools can identify and prevent cyber-attacks in real-time, helping organizations stay ahead of evolving threats. Real-world examples like **Darktrace** and **CrowdStrike** demonstrate how AI is being used to protect networks and endpoints, while companies like

PayPal and **Google** are leveraging AI to combat fraud and phishing attacks.

As AI continues to advance, its role in cybersecurity will expand, but so too will the challenges. Cybercriminals may begin using AI to enhance their attacks, leading to an ongoing AI arms race between attackers and defenders. Despite these challenges, AI is poised to play a crucial role in safeguarding digital infrastructure, and its collaboration with human experts will be key to securing the future of cyberspace.

CHAPTER 18: THE ROAD AHEAD: FUTURE TRENDS IN AI AND MACHINE LEARNING

Artificial intelligence (AI) and machine learning have made remarkable progress in the past decade, powering innovations in industries from healthcare to finance, transportation, and entertainment. As we look toward the future, AI's potential seems almost limitless. From the development of **Artificial General Intelligence (AGI)** to breakthroughs in fields like **space exploration** and **quantum computing**, the road ahead for AI promises to transform human life in ways we are only beginning to imagine. In this chapter, we'll explore the future trends in AI, including cutting-edge research, and examine real-world innovations that are paving the way for tomorrow's AI-driven world.

The Future Potential of AI: AGI and Beyond

Currently, most AI systems are **narrow AI**—designed to perform specific tasks, such as playing chess, recognizing images, or processing natural language. These systems are highly effective at what they do but are limited in their scope. The future of AI is largely focused on developing more advanced forms of intelligence, with the ultimate goal being **Artificial General Intelligence (AGI)**.

1. *What is AGI?*

Artificial General Intelligence (AGI) refers to a level of AI that can perform any intellectual task that a human can, with the ability to understand, learn, and apply knowledge across a broad range of subjects. Unlike narrow AI, which is specialized for a single task, AGI would possess the cognitive flexibility to handle multiple tasks, reason about new problems, and adapt to changing environments in ways that mirror human intelligence.

Characteristics of AGI

- **Generalized Learning**: AGI would not require vast amounts of data or specific training for every task. Instead, it would learn in a more human-like way, applying existing knowledge to new situations and adapting to different challenges.
- **Understanding and Reasoning**: AGI would possess the ability to reason about abstract concepts, make judgments, and understand complex cause-and-effect relationships.
- **Self-Improvement**: One of the most important aspects of AGI is that it would have the capacity to improve itself, identifying gaps in its own knowledge or

capabilities and autonomously seeking out ways to enhance its performance.

2. The Challenges of Developing AGI

The path to AGI is filled with challenges, both technical and philosophical. While AI researchers have made significant strides in developing narrow AI systems, AGI remains a distant goal. Here are a few of the key obstacles that need to be addressed:

- **Computational Power**: AGI would require enormous computational resources to process and understand vast amounts of information. While current advances in hardware (such as GPUs and TPUs) have accelerated AI development, AGI will likely require new breakthroughs in computational efficiency and hardware design.

- **Knowledge Representation**: Developing AGI requires figuring out how to represent and process knowledge in a way that enables machines to understand the world similarly to humans. This involves not just pattern recognition but the ability to reason, infer, and apply knowledge to new domains.

- **Ethical and Safety Concerns**: AGI raises profound ethical questions. If machines gain the ability to reason and make decisions independently, how do we ensure they act in ways that are aligned with human values? The potential risks associated with AGI, including loss of control or unintended consequences, require careful consideration.

3. AGI and Superintelligence: What Lies Beyond?

Some researchers speculate that the development of AGI could lead to **superintelligence**—an AI system that surpasses human intelligence in virtually every domain. Superintelligent AI could outperform humans in areas such as creativity, problem-solving, and decision-making, leading to significant technological advances. However, the implications of superintelligent AI also raise concerns about control and safety.

- **Positive Outcomes**: A superintelligent AI could solve many of humanity's greatest challenges, such as curing diseases, addressing climate change, or advancing space exploration.
- **Potential Risks**: Superintelligence also brings potential risks, including the possibility that AI could act in ways that are harmful to humanity, whether through unintended consequences or goals that diverge from human interests. Researchers in AI safety are working to develop frameworks to ensure that future AI systems remain aligned with human values.

Real-World Examples of Cutting-Edge Research and Innovation

While AGI remains an ambitious long-term goal, current AI research is producing impressive advancements that are bringing us closer to more general forms of intelligence. Here are some real-world examples of cutting-edge AI research and innovation.

1. OpenAI's GPT-4: The Evolution of Language Models

OpenAI's GPT-4 represents the next step in the evolution of large language models, building on the success of **GPT-3**, which set a new standard for natural language processing. GPT-4 is designed to understand and generate human-like text across a wide range of topics, from writing essays and poetry to answering complex questions.

Key Advancements in GPT-4

- **Improved Comprehension and Contextual Understanding**: GPT-4 is better at maintaining context over longer passages, allowing it to generate more coherent and relevant responses in conversation.

- **Cross-Domain Capabilities**: While GPT-3 could generate text in response to prompts, GPT-4 extends this by being able to handle more nuanced reasoning tasks, such as explaining complex scientific concepts or analyzing historical events.

- **Multimodal Abilities**: GPT-4 has the potential to integrate multiple forms of data (such as text, images, and audio), making it capable of processing more complex inputs and generating richer outputs.

2. AlphaFold: AI in Scientific Discovery

One of the most impactful breakthroughs in AI came with **DeepMind's AlphaFold**, an AI system that solved the decades-old problem of **protein folding**. AlphaFold demonstrated how AI could accelerate scientific discovery by accurately predicting the 3D structures of proteins based on their amino acid sequences.

The Significance of AlphaFold

- **Biological Understanding**: Protein folding is central to understanding how biological processes work at the molecular level. By accurately predicting protein structures, AlphaFold has the potential to revolutionize fields such as drug discovery, disease research, and synthetic biology.

- **Drug Discovery**: AlphaFold's predictions are helping scientists identify new targets for drugs, understand the mechanisms behind diseases, and develop more effective treatments.

- **Open Science**: DeepMind released AlphaFold's data and predictions to the global scientific community, providing access to more than **200 million protein**

structures. This democratization of knowledge has accelerated research in laboratories worldwide.

3. Neuralink: AI-Driven Brain-Computer Interfaces

Neuralink, a company founded by Elon Musk, is exploring the frontier of **brain-computer interfaces (BCIs)**, aiming to connect the human brain directly with AI systems. This technology has the potential to revolutionize medicine, communication, and even human cognition.

Applications of Brain-Computer Interfaces

- **Medical Applications**: BCIs could enable people with neurological conditions, such as paralysis or neurodegenerative diseases, to control computers, prosthetics, or other devices with their thoughts. This could dramatically improve the quality of life for individuals with disabilities.
- **Enhanced Cognition**: In the long term, BCIs may be used to enhance human intelligence by directly interfacing with AI systems, allowing people to process information faster or access knowledge instantaneously.

- **Communication**: BCIs could facilitate new forms of communication, allowing people to convey thoughts and emotions without the need for speech or text.

The Potential for AI in Space Exploration, Quantum Computing, and More

Looking ahead, AI has the potential to make significant contributions to fields like **space exploration**, **quantum computing**, and **climate change mitigation**. These are areas where AI can enable humanity to tackle challenges that are currently beyond our reach.

1. AI in Space Exploration

AI is already playing a key role in space exploration, and its importance will only grow as we venture further into the cosmos. From autonomous spacecraft to AI-powered rovers, the use of machine learning and AI in space missions is enabling new discoveries and capabilities.

AI-Powered Rovers and Spacecraft

- **Mars Rovers**: NASA's **Perseverance Rover**, currently exploring Mars, uses AI to navigate the planet's surface autonomously. AI systems allow the rover to avoid obstacles, identify interesting geological features, and prioritize its scientific objectives without needing constant human oversight.

- **Spacecraft Autonomy**: As space missions venture deeper into the solar system, real-time communication with Earth becomes less feasible due to the vast distances involved. AI is essential for enabling spacecraft to operate autonomously, making decisions about navigation, data collection, and system maintenance.

AI for Space Research

- **Exoplanet Discovery**: AI is being used to analyze vast datasets from space telescopes, identifying potential exoplanets (planets outside our solar system) by recognizing patterns in the data. Machine learning algorithms can sift through enormous amounts of information far faster and more accurately than human researchers.

- **Astronomical Data Processing**: The **Square Kilometre Array (SKA)**, a massive radio telescope project set to be operational in the coming years, will produce more data in a single day than the entire internet generates in the same period. AI will be essential for processing and analyzing this data to uncover new insights about the universe.

2. AI in Quantum Computing

Quantum computing represents the next frontier in computing power, with the potential to solve problems that are currently intractable for classical computers. **AI and quantum computing** are poised to complement each other in profound ways, with AI helping to optimize quantum algorithms and quantum computers potentially accelerating AI research.

The Synergy Between AI and Quantum Computing

- **Quantum AI**: Quantum computers could dramatically speed up machine learning algorithms by leveraging quantum properties such as superposition and entanglement. This could lead to breakthroughs in areas like cryptography, drug discovery, and climate modeling.
- **Optimization Problems**: Quantum computers excel at solving complex optimization problems—tasks that require finding the best solution among a vast number of possibilities. AI models, particularly those used in logistics, finance, and materials science, could benefit from quantum computing's ability to quickly process and analyze large datasets.

3. AI for Climate Change Mitigation

As climate change becomes an increasingly urgent global challenge, AI is being harnessed to help mitigate its impacts. From optimizing energy consumption to modeling the effects of climate interventions, AI can provide insights and solutions that were previously out of reach.

AI for Sustainable Energy

- **Smart Grids**: AI is helping to develop **smart grids**, which use machine learning to balance energy supply and demand more efficiently. By predicting when and where energy will be needed, AI can reduce waste and help integrate renewable energy sources like wind and solar into the grid.

- **Energy Optimization**: AI-driven algorithms are being used to optimize energy use in buildings, factories, and transportation systems, reducing greenhouse gas emissions and improving sustainability.

Climate Modeling

- **Environmental Monitoring**: AI is used to analyze data from satellites, weather stations, and ocean sensors to track changes in the Earth's climate. Machine learning models can predict future climate patterns, helping scientists and policymakers make more informed decisions about how to address climate change.

- **Carbon Capture**: AI is being applied to the development of carbon capture and storage technologies, which aim to remove carbon dioxide from the atmosphere and store it underground. AI can help optimize these systems, making them more efficient and cost-effective.

Conclusion

The future of AI holds immense promise, from the development of **Artificial General Intelligence (AGI)** to groundbreaking applications in space exploration, quantum computing, and climate change mitigation. While we are still far from realizing the full potential of AGI, current advancements in AI are already transforming scientific research, healthcare, communication, and industry. As AI continues to evolve, its capabilities will expand, opening up new possibilities for solving some of humanity's most pressing challenges.

Looking ahead, the road to AGI will require overcoming significant technical, ethical, and philosophical hurdles. However, the ongoing advancements in machine learning, hardware, and interdisciplinary collaboration are laying the foundation for future breakthroughs. Whether in space exploration, quantum computing, or the fight against climate change, AI will continue to play a pivotal role in shaping the future

CHAPTER 19: THE ROLE OF HUMANITY IN AN AI-DRIVEN WORLD

Artificial intelligence (AI) is rapidly reshaping our world, revolutionizing industries, driving technological breakthroughs, and transforming the way we live and work. Throughout this book, we've explored the foundations of AI, its applications across various fields, and the profound impact it will have on the future. As we move deeper into an AI-driven era, it's critical to reflect on the balance between the incredible benefits AI offers and the risks it presents. This final chapter will recap the key concepts we've covered, discuss the importance of managing AI's potential risks, and provide guidance on how readers can continue learning and staying informed about AI's ongoing developments.

Recap of Key Concepts

1. The Foundations of AI and Machine Learning

In the early chapters, we broke down **artificial intelligence (AI)** and **machine learning (ML)** into simple terms, explaining how these technologies allow machines to learn from data, make decisions, and solve problems. **Supervised learning**, **unsupervised learning**, and **reinforcement learning** were identified as the main types of machine learning, each serving different purposes, from recognizing patterns to teaching AI through rewards. We also explored **deep learning**, a powerful subset of machine learning that uses neural networks to model complex patterns in data, enabling breakthroughs in fields like image recognition, natural language processing, and game-playing.

2. AI's Role Across Industries

AI's transformative power has already made significant inroads into industries such as **healthcare**, **finance**, **transportation**, **entertainment**, and **education**. From assisting doctors with diagnoses to automating customer service and optimizing supply chains, AI's impact is pervasive. We explored how AI is making strides in key areas:

- **Healthcare**: AI systems like **IBM Watson** assist in diagnosing diseases, while AI-driven drug discovery platforms accelerate the creation of new treatments.
- **Finance**: AI enhances fraud detection, algorithmic trading, and personalized financial services through robo-advisors and automated tools.
- **Autonomous Vehicles**: AI powers self-driving cars, drones, and smart traffic systems, paving the way for safer, more efficient transportation.
- **Customer Service**: Chatbots and virtual agents, powered by AI, handle millions of customer

interactions daily, providing personalized service and reducing operational costs.

- **Creative Fields**: AI is now capable of generating art, music, and literature, demonstrating that machines can assist in creativity, from creating new musical compositions to helping write books.

3. Emerging Technologies and AI's Future

As AI continues to evolve, we explored future trends, such as the potential for **Artificial General Intelligence (AGI)**—AI that can perform any intellectual task a human can. Although AGI remains a distant goal, advances in areas like **quantum computing**, **brain-computer interfaces**, and **space exploration** are opening up new possibilities for AI. We also looked at AI's role in addressing global challenges like **climate change** and its potential applications in **scientific research** and **sustainability efforts**.

The Balance Between AI Benefits and Risks

AI's potential to solve problems and drive progress is enormous, but with great power comes great responsibility. As AI becomes more integrated into our lives, we must strike a balance between reaping its benefits and mitigating its risks.

1. Benefits of AI

The benefits of AI are vast and diverse. AI has the potential to improve healthcare outcomes, increase productivity, create new jobs, and lead to groundbreaking scientific discoveries. In daily life, AI can simplify tasks, offer personalized services, and enhance communication. From smart homes that adjust to our preferences to AI-powered digital assistants that help manage our schedules, AI is making life more convenient and efficient.

In business, AI is a powerful tool for optimizing operations, driving innovation, and making better decisions through data-driven insights. Companies that leverage AI are gaining a competitive edge, unlocking new revenue streams, and delivering more personalized customer experiences. On a global scale, AI could help address pressing issues like poverty, inequality, and environmental sustainability.

2. Risks and Ethical Challenges

While AI presents many benefits, it also comes with significant risks that must be managed carefully. These risks include:

- **Job Displacement**: As AI automates tasks across industries, there is a growing concern that it will lead to job displacement. While AI is expected to create new roles, particularly in tech-related fields, the transition may be challenging for workers whose jobs are at risk of automation. Managing this transition will require investments in education, reskilling, and social safety nets.

- **Bias and Discrimination**: AI systems are only as good as the data they are trained on. If the data reflects biases—

whether based on race, gender, or socioeconomic status—the AI system may unintentionally perpetuate these biases, leading to discriminatory outcomes. Ensuring fairness and transparency in AI algorithms is essential for creating equitable systems.

- **Privacy Concerns**: AI systems often require vast amounts of personal data to function effectively, raising concerns about privacy and data security. In particular, the widespread use of AI in facial recognition and surveillance poses significant risks to individual privacy and civil liberties.

- **Autonomous Systems and Safety**: Autonomous AI systems, such as self-driving cars and drones, have the potential to cause harm if they malfunction or make incorrect decisions. Ensuring the safety and reliability of these systems is critical, especially as they become more integrated into daily life.

- **The Control Problem**: As AI systems become more powerful and capable of making decisions independently, there is a growing concern about the **control problem**—the risk that highly intelligent AI systems could act in ways that are misaligned with human values or interests. Researchers are working to develop safeguards and ethical frameworks to ensure that AI systems remain under human control.

3. AI Ethics and Governance

Given these risks, it's essential to establish ethical frameworks and governance structures to guide the development and deployment of AI. Policymakers, researchers, and industry leaders must work together to ensure that AI is used responsibly and for the benefit of society.

Key areas of focus include:

- **Transparency and Accountability**: AI systems must be transparent in how they make decisions, particularly in high-stakes areas like healthcare, finance, and criminal justice. Clear accountability mechanisms should be in place to ensure that when AI systems make errors or cause harm, responsibility can be appropriately assigned.
- **AI Safety Research**: Researchers must continue to explore ways to make AI systems safe and reliable. This includes developing techniques for ensuring AI systems are robust, interpreting their behavior, and aligning them with human values.
- **Inclusive AI Development**: To prevent AI from exacerbating social inequalities, it's important to ensure that diverse perspectives are included in the development of AI systems. This includes involving ethicists, sociologists, and representatives from marginalized communities in the AI development process.

How Readers Can Continue Learning and Stay Informed About AI Developments

As AI continues to advance at a rapid pace, it's important to stay informed and engaged with the latest developments. Whether you're a student, a professional, or simply a curious individual, there are numerous ways to deepen your understanding of AI and keep up with new trends.

1. Online Learning Resources

There are a wealth of online courses and educational platforms that provide accessible and in-depth learning on AI and machine learning:

- **Coursera** offers courses from top universities like Stanford and MIT, covering AI fundamentals, machine learning, deep learning, and more.
- **Khan Academy** provides free lessons on AI and related topics like computer science and data analysis, making it a great resource for beginners.
- **edX** features courses from institutions like Harvard and Berkeley, focusing on AI research, algorithms, and ethics.

2. Follow AI Research and News

To stay informed about cutting-edge research, follow reputable sources of AI news and academic publications:

- **AI Research Papers**: Websites like **arXiv** and **Google Scholar** publish academic research papers on the latest AI breakthroughs. Keeping up with these publications is a great way to dive deeper into technical advancements.

- **AI News Platforms**: Websites like **TechCrunch**, **Wired**, and **MIT Technology Review** regularly report on AI innovations, startups, and ethical debates. Subscribing to these platforms can help you stay up-to-date on industry trends.

3. Participate in AI Communities

Joining AI-focused communities can be a great way to learn from others, share insights, and discuss ethical implications. You can find such communities online or through local meetups:

- **AI Forums and Discussion Boards**: Platforms like **Reddit**'s AI community and **Stack Overflow** are popular spaces for discussing AI-related questions and sharing resources.

- **Meetups and Conferences**: Attending AI conferences, such as **NeurIPS**, **ICML**, or **AI Expo**, allows you to hear from leading researchers and network with professionals in the field.

4. Stay Engaged with AI Ethics and Policy

As AI continues to reshape society, it's important to stay engaged with the ethical and policy discussions surrounding its use. Here are a few ways to do so:

- **Follow AI Ethics Research**: Read about AI ethics initiatives, such as **The Future of Humanity Institute**, **OpenAI**, and **AI Now Institute**, which explore the ethical, legal, and societal implications of AI.

- **Engage in Policy Discussions**: Track government efforts to regulate AI through initiatives like **AI legislation** and **global AI governance forums**. Understanding the regulatory landscape will help you stay informed about how governments and organizations are shaping AI's future.

Conclusion: Humanity's Role in an AI-Driven World

As we move forward in this AI-driven world, one thing is clear: AI is not a replacement for human ingenuity but a tool to augment and enhance our abilities. It holds the potential to solve many of our greatest challenges, from improving healthcare to addressing climate change and exploring new frontiers in space. However, the power of AI must be guided responsibly, with a commitment to ethics, fairness, and human values.

Humanity's role in an AI-driven world is to ensure that these technologies are developed and deployed in ways that benefit everyone. This requires a collective effort from researchers, policymakers, and everyday citizens to stay informed, ask critical questions, and engage with the ongoing conversation about the future of AI.

As you close this book, I encourage you to continue exploring the world of AI with curiosity, critical thinking, and a commitment to shaping a future where AI serves as a force for good. The road ahead is full of possibilities, and the role you play in that journey—whether as a learner, a creator, or an advocate—will help define the future of AI.

www.ingramcontent.com/pod-product-compliance
Lightning Source LLC
LaVergne TN
LVHW051324050326
832903LV00031B/3358